W9-BWE-055

CULTURE SMART!
INDIA

Becky Stephen

·K·U·P·E·R·A·R·D·

ISBN 978 1 85733 525 5
This book is also available as an e-book: eISBN 978 1 85733 540 8

British Library Cataloguing in Publication Data
A CIP catalogue entry for this book is available from the British Library

First published in Great Britain
by Kuperard, an imprint of Bravo Ltd
59 Hutton Grove, London N12 8DS
Tel: +44 (0) 20 8446 2440   Fax: +44 (0) 20 8446 2441
www.culturesmart.co.uk
Inquiries: sales@kuperard.co.uk

Distributed in the United States and Canada
by Random House Distribution Services
1745 Broadway, New York, NY 10019
Tel: +1 (212) 572-2844   Fax: +1 (212) 572-4961
Inquiries: csorders@randomhouse.com

Series Editor Geoffrey Chesler
Design Bobby Birchall

Printed in Malaysia

Cover image: *Fresco on the walls at Mandawa, Rajasthan.* © Fotolia.com

Images on these pages are reproduced under Creative Commons Attribution Share-Alike licenses 1.0, 2.0, 2.5, and 3.0: 15 © Matthew Laird Acred; 17 © Mamoon Mengal; 20 © Yann; 21 © Jen; 22 © Serge Duchemin; 29 © ampersandyslexia; 46 © Purshi; 48 © Ken Wieland; 62 © dhondusaxena; 94 © Biswarup Ganguly; 99 © Maria Krüger; 109 © Bala; 118 © michael clarke stuff; 119 © Hans A. Rosbach; 124 © Deepak; 128 © Grey Rocker; 129 © Dforest; 143: © Srisez

Images on the following pages are reproduced under Creative Commons Attribution 2.0 Generic license: 35 © Claude Renault; 41 © Steve Jurvetson; 63 © Vijay Bandari; 68: © Tejal Patel; 69 © Monjurul Hoque; 70 © Meenakshi Payal; 90 © Ananth BS; 97 © Naresh Dhiman; Page 101 © kawanet; 114 © Varun Shiv Kapur; 120 © Navin Thakur; 122 © Marc Shandro; 160 © counterclockwise

About the Author

BECKY STEPHEN is a writer, management consultant, and cross-cultural trainer for businesses and nonprofit organizations in Dubai, the UK, and the USA. After graduating with a Masters in Cross Cultural Studies from Fuller Theological Seminary, Pasadena, California, she developed and led cross-cultural and other training programs and events in the USA, India, Eurasia, and Europe, and headed the US division of a nonprofit organization responsible for Americans on long-term international assignments. She has written many articles and training materials on cross-cultural and spiritual issues.

Long fascinated by Indian culture and philosophy, Becky went to India in 1988 to study Hindi at Banaras Hindu University, Varanasi, and ended up living there for nearly five years. She currently lives in Dubai with her Indian husband and son.

**The Culture Smart! series is continuing to expand.
For further information and latest titles visit
www.culturesmart.co.uk**

The publishers would like to thank **CultureSmart!**Consulting for its help in researching and developing the concept for this series.

CultureSmart!Consulting creates tailor-made seminars and consultancy programs to meet a wide range of corporate, public-sector, and individual needs. Whether delivering courses on multicultural team building in the USA, preparing Chinese engineers for a posting in Europe, training call-center staff in India, or raising the awareness of police forces to the needs of diverse ethnic communities, it provides essential, practical, and powerful skills worldwide to an increasingly international workforce.

For details, visit www.culturesmartconsulting.com

CultureSmart!Consulting and **CultureSmart!** guides have both contributed to and featured regularly in the weekly travel program "Fast Track" on BBC World TV.

contents

contents

Map of India

introduction

India. The name instantly evokes associations and images in our minds. India has painted its colors on nearly every aspect of modern Western life. The food we eat, how we decorate our homes, what we wear, how we exercise, the movies we watch, the technology we use, and the religious options available to us have all been influenced by the many cultures and peoples of India. Indian languages have even entered our vocabulary: pundit, jodhpurs, and pajamas were Hindi words taken up by the British Raj; catamaran, pariah, and curry are Tamil contributions.

Seen from afar, perceptions of India may be based on scary headlines about terrorist attacks in urban centers; overwhelming statistics on population and snapshots of poverty; technological competition in the global market; exotic art forms; and ancient history. All this is true. But at its heart India is its people. Mother India's one billion "children" are as varied and colorful as the spice markets of Old Delhi. Each region, caste, and community has its own culture, reflecting unique histories shaped by conquest, creativity, and religion, expressed in distinct languages, social customs, art forms, and expectations of life.

Indian civilization has developed over five thousand years. Despite enormous changes in recent decades, in many ways it remains the same—a total sensory experience. The chaos and beauty of color and sound, the language shifts every ten miles, the household variations of spice and spiciness, the insistent smells of everyday life lived very much in public, and the invasion of personal space will challenge the most experienced traveler. But it is in surrender to your senses that you begin to embrace the essence of India and to understand its people.

As you experience India up close, you will begin to understand something of the seemingly infinite capacity of Indians to live with paradox. The spectacle of India's proud traditions and the Indians' love for their land is commingled with tensions and prejudices rooted in conquests and rivalries long past. Ancient temples decorated with bright colors and intricate sculptures may be plastered with signs advertising the latest technologies. You will smell the burgeoning slums that have been part of the rapid urbanization of the last century, and meet an affluent middle class that was nonexistent before the last few decades. You'll taste the metallic tang of pollution as your auto rickshaw darts through traffic, competing with delicious aromas steaming from the vats of street vendors.

Steeped in tradition, exceptionally fatalistic, and intensely passionate about their culture, the Indians are some of the most ingenious, adventurous, and creative people on the planet. Warm and friendly, most will respond to your interest in them and their country with generosity and genuine friendship. But they also have indelible ties to family and community that form boundary lines and determine decisions that do not always seem reasonable, or sometimes even ethical, to those looking on from the outside.

Visitors' responses to India can be as extreme as the people and places they encounter there. This book aims to make you aware of the basic values and behavioral norms, to show you how to navigate cultural differences and connect with real people, and to offer insights into the sometimes frustrating, but endlessly fascinating, place that is India.

Key Facts

Country Name	Republic of India	In Hindi, Bharatiya Ganarajya (Bharat)
Capital	New Delhi	Old Delhi (Shahjahanabad), in the heart of New Delhi, was the Mughal capital.
Most Populated Cities	Mumbai 16.4 million Kolkata 13.2 million Delhi 12.8 million Chennai 6.4 million Bangaluru 5.7 million	India has 44 cities with a population of more than 1 million.
Area	1,269,219 sq. miles (3,287,263 sq. km)	Seventh largest country in the world
Climate	Varies from tropical monsoon in the south to temperate in the north	Best times to visit are October to March, or September through November if visiting the Himalayas
Border Countries	Bangladesh, Bhutan, China, Myanmar, Nepal, Pakistan. There are 4,400 miles (7,000 km) of coastline.	Long-term border disputes with Pakistan
Government	Liberal democratic federal republic. Two houses of parliament: the upper Council of States (Rajya Sabha) and the lower House of the People (Lok Sabha)	The head of state, elected for a five-year term, is the President; the head of government the Prime Minister. There are 28 states and 7 union territories.
Population	1,166,079,217 (2009). Second largest in the world	Plus 25 million in the Indian Diaspora

Age Structure	Population below 15 yrs, 31%; below 25 yrs, 50%; below 35 yrs, 75%; below 65 yrs, 95%	
Life Expectancy	Male 65; female 67	
Ethnic Makeup	Indo-Aryan 72%; Dravidian 25%; Mongoloid and other 3%	
Religion	Hindus 80%; Muslims 13%; Christians 2.3%; Sikhs 1.9%; Buddhists 0.8%; Jains 0.4%; Parsees, Baha'is, Jews, and others 0.6%	
Languages	Hindi is the official language. There are 22 national languages and 1,652 other languages spoken.	English is widely spoken and recognized by the constitution as an associate national language.
Literacy	65.38%: males 75.96%; females 54.28%	Literacy among the young (15–24 yrs): 87% (m); 77% (f)
Gross Domestic Product	$3.26 trillion (2008)	Per capita: $3,100 (2009 est.)
Per Capita Income	$900	25% live below the poverty line.
Currency	Indian rupees (Rs.)	US $1 = Rs. 46.22 (2010)
Electricity	230 volts, 50 Hz	Round-prong plug required. Frequent blackouts and load shedding.
Video/TV	The British PAL system is used.	
Internet Domain	.in	
Telephone	India's country code is 91.	To dial out of India dial 00, followed by the country code.
Time	GMT + 5.5 hrs (winter)	GMT + 4.5 hrs (summer)

LAND &
PEOPLE

BOUNDARIES AND *BANDHAN*

Bounded by the Himalayas to the north, the Arabian Sea to the west, and the Bay of Bengal to the east, the immense peninsula of India sits on a separate tectonic plate from the rest of Asia, together with its neighbors, Pakistan and Bangladesh. It also shares borders with China, Nepal, Bhutan, and Myanmar (Burma).

Throughout history, outsiders have identified this vast country as a place set apart. The Greek historian Herodotus in the fifth century BCE first dubbed it "India," having heard of the land across the Indus or Sindhu River from Persian travelers. The Persians called it "Hindustan"—"land of the people of the Sindhu River." Mughal conquerors called the indigenous peoples "Hindus." "Hindustan" came into popular usage during the British Raj and is still widely used in India today.

Within its borders the linguistic, ethnic, political, religious, and topographical differences are mind-boggling. Nagaland in the northeast boasts mahogany and rattan forests, and a unique Christian history. Off India's shores to the west and east lie island territories—the sparsely inhabited coral atolls of the predominantly Muslim Lakshadweep, and the distinct peoples who live on the volcanic chain of the Andaman and Nicobar Islands. In between you'll find climate and geographic extremes inhabited by thousands of peoples and linguistic groups with rich and varied histories and traditions.

Despite this great diversity, Indians identify themselves as a single people—as Bharat. Found in the ancient texts of the *Rig Veda* and the *Bhagavad Gita*, as well as in ancient Tamil, the name "*Bharatam*" referred to the people of the Indian peninsula. Bound together by their history, a complex but common social structure, and shared cultural values, the people of the peninsula have developed a separate and strong identity. At Independence, "Bharat" was adopted as the official name of the new nation.

UNITED INDIA

Raksha Bandhan is a Hindu festival honoring the brother-sister relationship. On the day of the full moon in the Hindu month of Shravan, which falls in August, girls tie silk threads, or *rakhis* ("bonds of protection") on the wrists of brothers and those boys they see as brothers. *Rakhis* were used to demonstrate against partition and sectarian violence in Bengal in the run-up to Independence. Declaring to the British government that Bengal was "one and indivisible," people took an oath and tied the threads to one another's wrists, binding their lives together beyond the ties of blood and religious affiliation.

GEOGRAPHY AND CLIMATE

With the seventh-largest landmass in the world, India's geography ranges from the breathtaking Himalayas to scorching desert, to dense tropical forests, to expansive plains. Around 4,400 miles (7,000 km) of coast provide beautiful beaches, rocky cliffs, and marshlands. The Ganges River cuts through the dry northern plains to merge forces with Central and South Asia's major river, the Brahmaputra, or Yamuna, before pouring out into the Bay of Bengal. Rivers and tributaries, mostly flowing from the Himalayas, run through the subcontinent like veins. These waters bring both life and death to India. The Yamuna, a valuable waterway depositing enormous amounts of fertile soil, has also become a frequent source of unpredictable flooding.

India can be divided into five geographical regions: the Islands, the Coastal Plains, the Peninsular Plateau, the North Plains, and the North Mountains. There are three major seasons—summer, monsoon, and winter—but climate changes with geography. Tropical, subtropical, arid, and alpine zones can all be found within India's borders.

Kerala, in the southwest, is tropical, with heavy rainfall (80–160 inches, or 200–400 cm, a year) and temperatures averaging 82–90°F (28–32°C). The southern tip of India has Hawaii-like weather nearly all year-round. Most of the rest of the country is not as fortunate.

April to June is summer time: 90°F (32°C) is the average summer temperature, but the average in the deserts can reach 122°F (50°C) or even above. In spite of scorching temperatures and little rain in the arid regions of the west in the summer months, these areas support a rich variety of vegetation and animal life.

The Thar, or Great Indian Desert, covering much of Rajasthan and parts of Gujarat, and the Himalayas in the north, both affect India's climate. Blocking the cold winds from central Asia, the Himalayas guarantee warmer temperatures than India would otherwise experience. The Thar attracts monsoon winds, ensuring the annual arrival of heavy rain across the subcontinent.

The north is a place of extremes: bone-chilling temperatures in winter give way to the scorching Loo wind in summer, when life is difficult for all who work or travel there. As June moves into July and August, heat and humidity rise to unbearable heights. A sigh of relief is heard when the monsoon finally breaks, with often awe-inspiring thunderstorms, sheets of rain, and overflowing rivers. From September to November, the monsoons wane in the west, drenching the east as winter approaches.

Winter in India, from December to February, is relatively dry and cool. Temperatures are, on the average, 50–60°F (10–15°C). Southern regions are warmed by the surrounding waters of the Indian Ocean, the Bay of Bengal, and the Arabian Sea. Rain is never long gone in some places in the northeast, which annually receive 394 inches (1,000 cm) of rain. For those interested in a true winter experience, parts of India do see snow. Himachal Pradesh, Uttaranchal, and Shimla, in the north, are known for their ski resorts.

THE PEOPLE

At 1.16 billion, India has the second-largest population in the world. With 17 percent of the earth's population and still growing, it promises to overtake China.

Though the urban population has multiplied elevenfold during the last century, 70 percent of Indians still live in villages. Migration to the cities continues to increase due to loss of lands and crops caused by flood and drought, coupled with a desire for better education and work opportunities. Cities of a million are considered towns in this country where the major cities of Delhi, Mumbai, and Kolkata have populations of more than ten million.

Cities continue to attract villagers desperate for a better life, but most rural migrants find themselves joining the immense slum populations and living in absolute poverty. In 2007, India ranked 126th on the United Nations' Human Development Index, which measures not only a country's economics, but its social, health, and educational conditions.

Language and Literacy

India is a linguist's paradise, with more than 1,600 languages, including the two classical languages of Sanskrit and Tamil. There are twenty-two official languages. Hindi is the official national language, and English serves as the predominant language for business and higher education.

Indians value education highly. According to a 2001 census, 95 percent of rural children have access to primary education, but 50 percent of those in the village drop out by the time they are twelve, or when their marriage is arranged. While south India has government-funded education until age sixteen, in the north this is not the case. India's literacy rate has continued to climb, from 51 percent twenty years ago to more than 65 percent. There is still a drastic difference between north and south, however, characterized by Kerala's 91 percent compared to that of Bihar, with 47 percent. And there are the expected variations between urban (80 percent) and rural (59 percent), and between male (76 percent) and female (54 percent), with urban women having twice the literacy of village women.

Religion

More than 80 percent of the population are registered as Hindus. And, although only 13 percent of Indians are

Muslim, India has the third-largest Muslim population in the world (the largest for a non-Muslim majority country). The remainder is made up of Christians mainly living in the south and the northeast (2.3 percent), Sikhs, typically found in Punjab (1.9 percent), Buddhists (0.8 percent), and Jains (0.4 percent). Jews, Zoroastrians, Baha'is, and others together comprise 0.6 percent.

The introduction of secularism in the last century was not meant to erase or replace religion in this profoundly spiritual country, but to win independence from the British and promote the political unification of culturally distinct kingdoms and peoples.

A BRIEF HISTORY
Ancient Indus (c. 3300–1500 BCE)
India's ancient civilization was born in the Indus River Valley, in the northwest region of the subcontinent, and flourished during the Bronze Age. The people of the valley, the Harappans, lived in multistoried brick homes with sewers, wells, and trash chutes, in well-laid-out towns. They developed metallurgical techniques to produce bronze, lead, tin, and copper. Grain was the currency of exchange and taxation. Symbols have been found that are thought to be an early Indus script.

Vedic Period (c. 1500–500 BCE)
It was in this valley that the Aryans first surfaced in Indian history. It is still debated whether the "Noble Ones," as they called themselves, migrated from Eurasia or arose as the indigenous culture of the Indus Valley. Whatever their origin, they settled in villages across North India and the plains of the Ganges, establishing Vedic civilization. Essentially tribal, these seminomadic people lived off the land, and introduced their religious beliefs of multiple

gods and goddesses who were worshiped and appeased through fire and ritual.

The Aryans established absolute monarchies and a hierarchy of nobility in the north. What became the Hindu caste system originated during this period, as kings assigned specific duties to individuals, who passed these responsibilities on to their heirs. Soon education and occupation were determined by birth.

As the Aryan kings occupied more territories, the Dravidians, an indigenous population predating the rise of the Aryans, were pushed south.

Many religious texts were created and passed on during this era. The *Vedas* (Sanskrit, "knowledge"), after which this period is named, laid the foundations of Hinduism and other major features of Indian culture.

The four *Vedas* took shape through oral tradition from 1500 BCE and were codified in 600 BCE. The philosophical *Upanishads*, the *Bhagavad-Gita*, and the *Mahabharata*, the longest epic poem ever written, all sprang from this period. The *Laws of Manu*, recorded in Sanskrit, prescribes rules of life for Hindus and solidified the castes into the four main strata that characterize India's social structure today.

In the fifth century BCE, a prince of the Shakya clan, Siddhartha Gautama, attained "Enlightenment," becoming known as the Buddha, or Enlightened One, and founded the religion of Buddhism. At the same time, Vardhamana Mahavira preached what was later to become Jainism.

As the sixteen Great Kingdoms, or *Maha Janapadas*, arose across the Indo-Gangetic plain, India experienced its second major period of urbanization.

Persian Empire (500–350 BCE)
The Persian king, Cyrus the Great, conquered India's northwestern region in 538 BCE. Eighteen years later, his son-in-law, Darius the Great (520 BCE), consolidated the rule of the Persians over the Indian subcontinent for the

next two hundred years. Persian political systems influenced future forms of government on the subcontinent, including those of the Mauryan dynasty.

Alexander the Great (327–323 BCE)

The conquering Macedonian king, Alexander the Great, crossed into India in 327 BCE to be welcomed by Ambhi, king of Taxila in western Punjab. At war with his eastern and northern neighbors, Ambhi hoped to enlist Alexander's aid against his enemies. Aid him he did. After fierce battles, Alexander vanquished every tribe, confederation, and king on his quest to reach Asia.

Once they had reached the Beas River (a tributary of the Ganges), Alexander's exhausted and disgruntled troops pressed him to head home. Turning back just nineteen months after he had entered India, Alexander left deputies to govern the Indian provinces.

Two years after Alexander's death in 323 BCE, these governors abandoned their posts and divided his empire among themselves. But when Seleucus I Nicator (the Conqueror) decided to recover the lost Indian lands in 305 BCE, he found his way blocked by Chandragupta Maurya, an exiled and possibly illegitimate son of the Magadha royal family. As Chandragupta proved too powerful to defeat, Seleucus made an alliance with him.

The Great Mauryan Empire (322–185 BCE)

The Mauryan Empire, regarded as the greatest in Indian history, dominated the subcontinent during the fourth and third centuries BCE. Its founder, Chandragupta Maurya, united the Empire; his son, Bendusara, expanded it by force over most of the subcontinent; and his grandson, Ashoka, made it great.

On learning of Alexander's death and the fragmentation of his empire, Chandragupta led a band of guerrillas in overthrowing King Dhama Nanda of Magadha in eastern

India and slaughtering the royal family. He conquered the North West Frontier and most of Afghanistan, and created an empire that extended from the Bay of Bengal in the east to the Arabian Sea and Persia in the west.

Chandragupta Maurya ruled for twenty-four years. His reign was not a benevolent one. This new emperor lived in such fear of assassination that he slept in a different room each night to confuse his enemies. He gave up his throne toward the end of his life and embraced Jainism. He was succeeded by his son, and then his grandson, Ashoka.

Ashoka the Great (273-232 BCE)
Ashoka the Great, born in 304 BCE, was emperor of all of the Indian subcontinent—or nearly all. His decision to extend his rule to the unconquered kingdom of Kalinga on the Bay of Bengal brought about a conversion of the man and his empire.

The carnage of war shook Ashoka. Turning to the teachings of Buddha, he set aside his weapons to put on the robes of a Buddhist monk.

This "Emperor of Emperors" effected reforms including the outlawing of animal sacrifice, the religious education of his people, and sending Buddhist missionaries to the Greeks and into the Near East. His impact on Indian history is such that Indian's national emblem, the Lion of Sarnath, and the wheel on the Indian flag known as the Ashoka Chakra, were both taken from his reign.

Between the two great empires of Maurya and Gupta, India was ruled regionally. It was in this in-between time, around 52 CE, that the apostle Thomas is said to have visited India, planting the seeds of Indian Christianity.

The Golden Age of the Guptas (320–550 CE)
Chandragupta I founded the Gupta dynasty; but the
Golden Age of India began when Chandragupta II rose
to power fifty years later, providing a stability through
military might that enabled science, art, literature,
and religion to reach their zenith.

Scholars of the day included the astronomer
Aryabhatta, who is said to have been the first to
conceptualize "zero." The exchange of ideas and
knowledge, especially religious, was actively
sought with China through a kind of
missionary exchange. The Gupta Empire
was also politically open, developing
diplomatic contacts in south Asia, Indonesia,
Persia, Greece, and Rome. As religious,
diplomatic, and trade relationships expanded,
the culture of the Gupta Empire was spread.

As is the fate of all empires, the Gupta Empire
weakened. When the Huns from Central Asia attacked in
450 CE, it could not hold them back. After the death of the
last Gupta, Bhanugupta, in 570, the Gupta Empire came to
a close. Once again India was ruled by smaller kingdoms
and remained divided until the Muslim invasions in 1000.

The Classical Age of the North and South Kingdoms
(647–1200)
Different empires dominated north and south, and
were frequently at war with each other. Although three
dynasties, known as the Rajputs, fought for control of
the north, art and the religions of Hinduism, Buddhism,
and Jainism still flourished during the Classical Age.

Another culture was growing in the rich soil of the
south, developing an art, literature, and architecture
distinctly its own. The Dravidians, driven south by the
Aryans long ago, now ruled kingdoms in India's southern
regions and expanded and controlled vast overseas

empires in Southeast Asia. They traded spices with the Roman Empire and Southeast Asia. The sciences and mathematics, as well as religion and philosophy, developed under the rule of these kings.

The Delhi Sultanate and the Beginning of Colonization (1200–1500)

For centuries Muslims from the north and west had made their way to India. Some came for riches, others to spread Islam; but most noted in history are those who came to rule. In a pattern that became familiar to India, Muslim traders arrived before Muslim invaders.

Delhi was captured in 1192 from the Rajput Hindu king Prithvi Raj Chauhan by Muhammed of Ghor, a Muslim general from what is today Afghanistan. Ghor founded the first of a series of dynasties to rule as the Delhi Sultanate.

During the reign of the Delhi Sultans many north Indian Hindus and Buddhists converted to Islam. The Sultans eventually controlled much of south India as well. In 1351 the south regained its independence as a Hindu state. Central India, too, rebelled, becoming a separate, though still Islamic, state. The Delhi Sultanate ended with the Mongol invasion of Timur in 1398.

Seafaring explorers from both China and Europe began to make their way to India. The Portuguese explorer Vasco da Gama was commissioned to find a sea route to India in 1497. Soon the Portuguese, Dutch, British, and French had set up trading posts on India's west coast.

These traders turned the rivalry of the warring kingdoms to their advantage, setting up not only trading posts but also political stakes across the land. By the end of the era of the Delhi Sultanate, the British had acquired all the European colonized territories in India except for French Pondicherry and Chandernagore, Dutch Tranvancore, and Portuguese Goa, Daman, and Diu.

The Great Mughal Empire (1526–1761)
In 1526, local Indian nobles, angered by Ibrahim Shah Lodi, the Sultan of Delhi, took revenge by inviting the Uzbek descendant of Genghis Khan, Zahir ud-din Muhammad Babur, ruler of Kabul, to invade Delhi and Agra. These nobles unwittingly helped Babur to usher in the Islamic Mughal Empire that would rule northern India for two hundred years.

Akbar the Great (1542–1605)
Jalaluddin Muhammad Akbar, known as Akbar the Great, ascended the throne when he was only thirteen years old. This grandson of Babur, seeking tolerance and peace, created new alliances and put an end to laws that penalized non-Muslims. Akbar was so serious about spiritual matters that he formed his own syncretic religion, *Din-i-ilahi* ("Divine Faith"), which died with him.

A great patron of the arts, Akbar enlarged the collections of Mughal art and literature and was responsible for the creation of the first "prefab" buildings. North Indian art and architecture were transformed as the Mughals built palaces, forts, and monumental tombs. Shah Jahan, most famous for his architectural wonders of the Red Fort, Jama Masjid, and the Taj Mahal, was Akbar's son. The Mughal Empire declined following the death of Shah Jahan's son, Aurangzeb, who ruled with a heavy hand, demolishing Hindu temples and reinstating taxation on non-Muslims.

Power was again decentralized as lesser kingdoms unsuccessfully sought to replace the Mughals. When the British government took control of India from the East India Company in 1858, more than a hundred kings were found to be issuing coins as the "Mughal Emperor."

The East India Company and Colonial India (1600–1947)
The East India Company was granted a charter by Queen Elizabeth I of England in 1600 with the aim of securing exclusive trading rights with India. The Mughal emperor Jahangir led the way in opening India's door to the Company in 1617. Sixty years later, when Siraj-ud-Doula, the Nawab of Bengal, refused to follow suit, the Company formed a private army, led by Robert Clive, and defeated the Nawab and his French allies. Clive was appointed as the East India Company's first Governor of Bengal in 1757. The Company created a trade monopoly in Bengal, introducing the Permanent Settlement, a land taxation system set up on a feudal-like structure. From 1772 to 1785 Warren Hastings, the Governor General of Bengal, raised a native army and pursued expansionist policies. By 1818 the Company controlled most of India.

Among the sepoys—Hindu and Muslim soldiers serving in the Company's three armies—growing discontent with British rule culminated in open rebellion in 1857 ("The Indian Mutiny"). The insurgents called on Bahadur Shah Zafar, the emperor in Delhi, to lead them. After a slow start the British eventually captured Delhi and conquered all the rebel strongholds. Bahadur Shah Zafar, the last of the Mughal emperors, who led this "First War of Independence," was exiled to Burma and his family line was extinguished. The British Crown now took direct control of India, making it the greatest of its colonies.

The British Raj ("reign") lasted from 1858 to 1947. It included areas directly administered by Britain and semiautonomous princely states ruled by Indian rulers under the ultimate authority of the British Crown.

In the south, Veerapandiya Kattabomman, a Tamil tribal chieftain, stood against the British Empire by refusing to pay taxes. A confrontational meeting with the tax collector turned into armed conflict. When Veerapandiya saw defeat was imminent, he fled with his forces, only to be captured and hanged on a tamarind tree for treason.

In the course of the nineteenth century, the British developed the country's economic, legal, and educational infrastructure, but skewed the economy to serve their own interests, as conquerors do. Imperial rule was a mixture of paternalism and racism, and in 1885 the Indian National Congress was founded in Bombay to counter the more repressive aspects of the Raj. By the 1940s India's huge contribution of troops and treasure to Great Britain's war effort, in both the First and the Second World Wars, had changed the way Indians perceived their situation.

The Indian Independence Movement (1940s)

Mohandas Karamchand Gandhi (1869–1948), who became known as the "Father of India," was one of many who sought India's independence from the British. At first the *Mahatma* ("Great Soul") campaigned for equality and civil rights within the Raj, until it became clear that his ideals could not be realized unless there were freedom from foreign domination. He joined together with other, passionate leaders such as Jawaharlal Nehru, secretary of the Indian National Congress, to create a national movement that would roll over India like a wave, pushing the British out by the power of mass nonviolent action.

The revolution that began to brew in the 1920s was not wholly nonviolent. Subash Chandra Bose broke away from Congress and during the Second World War, with Japanese help, organized the anti-British Indian National Army. The executed young revolutionary Bhagat Singh became a celebrated Indian martyr. These and many other great and small men and women fanned into flames the freedom movement that culminated in India's independence in 1947.

Bharat's Birth Pangs (1948–91)

No longer able to sustain its rule over India, Britain made a virtue of necessity and determined to concede its independence. In 1946 elections were called, in which the Congress Party won eight of the eleven provinces. But now the history of conflict between Muslims and Hindus on the subcontinent raised its head as the Muslim minority feared rule by a Hindu government. Intercommunal violence broke out. The Muslim League, led by Muhammad Ali Jinnah, called for an independent Muslim state. Partition, or separation of Pakistan from India, was Britain's parting gift.

The last British Viceroy, Lord Louis Mountbatten, speeded up the process with the imposition of a deadline for partition. On August 15, 1947, India became a sovereign state, and Pakistan was created from the Muslim majority areas. Twelve million Muslims, Hindus, and Sikhs began the largest migration in modern history, uprooting families and leaving properties to move to what they hoped would be a safe land ruled by their own people. The riots that broke out during the exodus to east and west left half a million dead.

Another shock wave hit the country when, on January 30, 1948, Gandhi, who had loudly opposed partition, was assassinated by a young Hindu nationalist, angered by his call for a united India for Muslims and Hindus.

Jawaharlal Nehru was the first prime minister of the new self-governing democracy. He was succeeded by Lal Bahadur Shastri, who faced ongoing conflict with Pakistan over Indian-held Kashmir before meeting with Pakistan's president to sign a no-war declaration following the Indo–Pakistani War in 1965.

Nehru's daughter, Indira Gandhi, became prime minister following his death in 1966. She presided over India's victory in the second Indo–Pakistani War, which resulted in the establishment of Bangladesh, formerly East Pakistan, as a separate nation, in 1971.

Another bomb burst when Mrs. Gandhi was found guilty of electoral fraud in 1975. Her response was to declare a state of emergency and impose authoritarian rule for nineteen months. She imprisoned a thousand political opponents and began a mandatory birth-control program to sterilize the mentally retarded and large populations of villagers, resulting in more than seven million vasectomies.

Not surprisingly, Mrs. Gandhi's government lost the election following the state of emergency, but she returned to power three years later. In 1984, Indira Gandhi was assassinated by her Sikh bodyguards in retaliation for the government's attack on the Sikhs' Golden Temple earlier that year.

In the tradition of India's great dynasties, Rajiv Gandhi, her second son, immediately, if reluctantly, stepped into his mother's place. Accused of corruption, his government collapsed in 1989. While running for election in 1991, Rajiv's last act was to greet a young woman who had seemingly come to touch his feet. The bomb blast from that suicide bomber, a Tamil Tiger sympathizer, was seen around the world and left India reeling.

Bharat the Great (1991–present)
The new millennium is witnessing great transformation in the culture and global influence of Bharat. India has become an economic powerhouse in the world economy. During the tenure of P. V. Narasimha Rao as prime minister in the early 1990s, extensive financial reforms were made by his finance minister, Manmohan Singh, leading to rapid economic growth.

Singh became known as the Father of Indian Economic Reform and went on to be elected prime minister in 2004 and again in 2009. He has reduced government deficits, launched large-scale rural job programs, provided debt relief to farmers, and created economic policies and tax reforms that have changed the economic climate.

India has become a nuclear power. In 2006 it signed a nuclear agreement with the USA, giving it access to civilian nuclear technology, American expertise, and nuclear fuel, with India promising to separate civilian and military nuclear programs and be subject to permanent international inspections. Two years later, the USA began nuclear trade with India; and in 2009 Russia agreed to supply India with US $700 million worth of uranium.

GOVERNMENT AND POLITICS

India is the world's largest democracy. A republic, it consists of twenty-eight states and six union territories and the New Capital Territory of Delhi. Historically the central government has had greater sway than the states; but the political, economic, and social reforms of the 1990s have increased the power of the states.

The Executive branch consists of the president, the vice president, and the Council of Ministers, headed by the prime minister. The president, as head of state, is elected for a five-year term by an electoral college. The prime minister is appointed by the president and is subordinate to the legislative branch of the lower house of parliament.

The Legislature consists of two houses of parliament, or Sansad: the upper Rajya Sabha (States Council) and the lower Lok Sabha (People's House). Rajya Sahba members are elected by states for a six-year term. Lok Sabha members are elected by the popular vote of individual constituencies and serve a five-year term.

The judiciary is headed by a Chief Justice, and includes twenty-one High Courts and the Supreme Court. The Supreme Court has the power to make laws and to overturn laws made by states that it deems to be unconstitutional.

Political parties in India are as numerous as Hindu gods, with dozens of state-recognized and hundreds of unrecognized regional parties competing for election. States have their own governments. When a party is recognized by four states, it automatically becomes a national party. Currently there are seven national parties: India National Congress

(INC), Nationalist Congress Party (NCP), Bharatiya Janata Party (BJP), Bahujan Samaj Party (BSP), Communist Party of India (Marxist) (CPI(M)), the Communist Party of India (CPI), and the Rashtriya Janata Dal (RJD).

Despite the complexities of Indian politics and the variance in levels of education, every Indian can explain how their government works and give an opinion about current affairs. Newspapers, radio, and television are part of everyday life, and not just for entertainment. With the rise of computer technology and access to the Internet, the Web, too, has become a vital source of global political information. For Indians, talking politics is like breathing.

Indians are passionate about their politics and dumbfounded by anyone who is not. The zeal and power seen in India's political history is still visible today in spontaneous political rallies that often combust into violent riots and in the high turnout at voting polls. Since Mahatma Gandhi's famous near-death fasts to bring attention to the plight of outcastes or to stop violent conflicts, many Indians have been willing to sacrifice their lives in an effort to persuade those who have the power to effect change.

TALKING POLITICS

Indians will no doubt inquire about your political views, as a foreigner. As in all new situations, the best starting posture is mouth firmly closed, ears, eyes, and mind wide-open. If you choose to engage, you may feel as if the whole room shares your opinion. They won't. But contradicting guests does not happen in India.

On the rare occasion you are openly challenged, don't be defensive. You may have just discovered someone who has the potential to be a true cultural guide. Cherish that relationship.

THE ECONOMY

For four decades India's economic growth was stunted by ideologically inspired policy restrictions and political corruption. Attempts to embrace aspects of capitalism while holding on to Nehru's socialism failed to bring the hoped-for social and economic results. When the Soviet Union, India's major trading partner, collapsed and the Gulf War caused oil prices to skyrocket, India faced a financial crisis of bailout proportions.

Manmohan Singh's reforms catapulted India into becoming the world's fastest-growing economy. GDP continued to grow throughout the world recession of 2008–09. In fact, the IT sector grew 20 percent that year. The stability of India's economy is due in part to the fact that 55 percent of it is still based on agriculture, and is primarily focused on domestic, rather than export, markets.

With the third-largest purchasing power on the planet after the USA and China, India is predicted to surpass them in the next twenty to thirty years. The burgeoning Indian middle class has its eye on the prize, and the education, networks, and resources to grab hold of it.

The New Middle Classes

Indians globally own 1 percent of the world's wealth. While 95 percent of Indian assets are invested in property, today's middle class is buying a different kind of lifestyle. There are 25 million nonresident Indians, all over the world.

Highly educated young Indians, with entrepreneurial vision and motivation, are marketing themselves globally. Inside and outside the country, India's under-forties look much like any well-to-do Westerners, from their designer-label jeans to their European vacations. With a predicted increase in spending power by a factor of seven within the next fifteen years, this generation is already shaping spending habits in India.

Their parents bought gold in the form of jewelry as a way of saving. But jewelry is becoming fashion, not fortune, as they invest their wealth in different ways. With the increase of discretionary income, purchases are based on choice and convenience, not just need. As dual-income couples become the norm in the city, so are supermarkets and packaged food. Cars that were once status symbols are now affordable by lower-middle-class families.

There's another new trend. Indians who once moved to the West to find work and wealth are returning to India. The shortage of IT professionals, engineers, and managers today means greater opportunity for employment and advancement inside India. The move "back home" has been driven by factors such as the cost of living, social and education concerns for children, family support, and the recent People of Indian Origin (PIO) and Overseas Citizen of India (OCI) options for those with US and other passports. The shift in India's economy and the openness to entrepreneurs makes the grass look greener on the South Asian side of the fence.

India has produced brilliant innovations in computer engineering and marketing. Indian-based technical support and software development is commonplace among the Big Boys of technology, from Microsoft and Google to Hewlett-Packard and IBM. Now Indian service-provider companies see the opportunity to shift from serving major companies to competing with them.

For centuries India has been known for its exports. "Made in India" received a boost in a 2009 policy aimed at doubling India's export of goods and services by 2014. Individual Indian entrepreneurs are making an impact on how we all do business, as well as on the global economy.

Experts predict that India will soon be the fastest-growing economy. The 2008 Asia–Pacific Wealth Report states that India is one of the fastest-growing "high net worth" populations, with both GDP and stock markets performing well above the global average. Goldman Sachs forecasts that by 2050 its economy will be in second place, just behind China's. Yet bleak poverty still plagues this country.

The Widening Divide

It is estimated that the average Indian income will double by 2020. But that is not saying much when the per capita income is only US $900 and 700 million are living on $2 a day or less. The poverty rate is declining barely more than 1 percent per annum. India has the highest concentration of poor on the planet, a fact made all the more dismal by the statistics related to children: it has the highest malnutrition rate of young children (46 percent of those under the age of three, based on 2007 figures); and despite the absence of famine, half of India's children are underweight—twice the rate of sub-Saharan Africa.

Despite a high infant mortality rate, India has a growing population. With more than 1 billion people and a growth rate of 1.4 percent in 2009, the strain on education and social structures could lead to demoralization and economic decline.

The labor force is second only to China in size; there are now 500 million Indians of working age. Many live without the means to feed their families, much less educate their children, or provide daughters with dowries. Tens of thousands of men and women, mostly unskilled laborers, are duped by promises of good jobs and a secure income to travel abroad, only to discover when they reach their destination that they are effectively enslaved, without access to funds, friendly governments, or the families they had hoped to provide for.

India's chronic social challenges could sabotage all promise of prosperity in the future. Yet the abundance of natural resources and the resourcefulness of India's people should not be underestimated.

chapter two

VALUES & ATTITUDES

A SENSE OF IDENTITY

Indians have a passionate sense of belonging. One could categorize this as nationalism, and sometimes it is, but these feelings are not primarily about India as a political entity. Indian identity is fashioned by history, community, and family. The subcategories and subcultures of language, caste, state, and religion *are* India.

The answer to the question "Who am I?" goes much deeper than "I am an Indian," and far broader than "I am me." Indians define themselves by history ("I am an Anglo-Indian"), by religion ("I am a Sikh"), caste ("I am a Nadar"), people group ("I am Assamese"), state ("I am Tamilian"), language ("I am a Malayalee"), or any number of categories that may not exist in other cultures. To attempt to paint them with a single brush would be to fail to grasp the extraordinary complexity of this people.

There are, however, shared values that transcend these divisions, giving Indians a common culture and enabling all of these distinct groups to say together, "I am Indian."

HIERARCHY

Hierarchy is inescapable in India. Everything and everyone is ranked, up or down, from everything and everyone else. Your place in the social order determines how others treat you, what is expected of you, what you can accomplish, and where you can go in the world and in life.

Look at where people sit. Literally. Chairs are offered to people of consequence. Though this does not apply in urban settings where people congregate, such as in a restaurant, it is not unusual to enter a room and see a few "big men" seated on the available chairs and everybody else sitting on the floor. You may not be able to tell the difference between "high" and "low," but they can. And everyone knows their place.

This is true within families, too. Language illustrates family hierarchy, structured according to age and gender. In many contexts, a wife does not address her husband by name, as an equal, but may refer to him as "Daddy," or another relational term. Children address older siblings using specific suffixes, as in Tamil's "Annan," elder brother, or Hindi's "Didi," big sister. From birth Indians learn who they are in the pecking order of family, community, and society. Outside the family, hierarchy in the community is often acknowledged using respectful familial titles, such as "Bhai," brother, in north India, or the ubiquitous English terms "Aunty" or "Uncle."

Caste

"Caste" was originally a Hindu concept, referring to the distinct hereditary groups ranked in the social order.

Theologically, the four original castes, or *varnas*, sprang from the body of the creator god, Brahma: Brahmins or priests from the mouth, Kshatriyas or rulers from the arms, Vaishyas, merchants and farmers, from the thighs, and Shudras, the artisans and servants, from the feet. Initially based on occupation, these *varnas* are now rigid categories dictating value and life possibilities not just for Hindus, but for all Indians.

> **Each finger should have its own width.**
> *Tamil proverb*

Caste groups are too numerous to name. Thousands of castes and subcastes are found across India. Regional and religious subcultures have their own clearly discernible caste delineations. A person's name, birthplace, and physical features, including skin color, can be indicators of caste.

Some people will tell you that caste has been abolished, and that's true on paper and on the surface. There have been significant improvements in educational and vocational opportunity for "lower castes" and "out castes." (Though to take advantage of those opportunities, official forms must record your caste.) In urban settings, caste appears to matter less. On jam-packed public buses you don't know whom you're rubbing shoulders with. In busy restaurants you have no control over who cooks your food or who sits at the next table. On the street people do not wear caste badges; the clothing that once signified one's caste is no longer worn. Many Indians have modified their names to make their caste unrecognizable. In these contexts, class distinction, based on education and income, becomes predominant.

But caste consciousness is alive and well. Every Indian walks around with a radar born of personal and cultural history, scanning for clues that indicate where they fit in the puzzle that is the caste system. Only with conscious thought and intent will anyone become "too friendly" with someone of lesser rank. Even for those who are less observant of caste protocols in daily life, when important life decisions such as marriage must be made, the importance of caste becomes very evident.

There are those who live outside caste. The 16 percent of the population who are too low to be considered part of the caste system are called, variously, "Dalit," "Untouchable,"

"Harijan," and "Scheduled." In the 1950s Dr. B. R. Ambedkar, a Dalit political leader, converted from Hinduism to Buddhism in protest against the caste system. Millions have subsequently followed his example, converting to Buddhism or Christianity to escape the clutches of caste. Though, theologically, Buddhists believe all distinctions to be unreal, and Christians affirm the unity of all believers, in real life caste and social hierarchy are present in all India's religions. Not allowed to be truly out of caste, the Dalits have in effect become a fifth caste, demonstrating the hold of the system.

Class

Class is linked to caste. There are three main classes: Forward (higher castes), Backward (middle and lower castes), and Dalit. Class often forms the basis of political groups and alliances. There is a general correlation between caste and prosperity: the higher the caste, the more options the individuals have had for education, connection, and advancement.

> **Whoever owns the stick owns the buffalo.**
> *Hindi proverb*

A newcomer to India's class system—the fast-growing middle class—is reshaping Indian categories and definitions of "class." The National Council of Applied Economic Research defines "middle class" as those who have a purchasing power of US $20–120,000 per annum, that is, 6 percent of the population. If the criterion is expanded to include consumers who can afford a phone, a car, and color TV, 20 percent of India's population fall within the parameters of "middle class." It is estimated that the purchasing power of this 20 percent will increase elevenfold over the next fifteen years.

This upwardly mobile group of people from up and down the traditional caste and class hierarchies is driven to create a better future for themselves and their children. Members of the new middle class—who may be large-scale farmers, owners of midsized businesses, or IT department managers—are using every available opportunity to generate wealth, in ways unknown to previous generations.

One unforeseen outcome of becoming middle class has been the tension between communal and individual identity and fulfillment. Raised to see themselves and make decisions as part of a family, caste, and community, many in the middle are caught unawares by the new opportunities for self-expression, and self-centeredness, that come with the means and with broader professional and personal relationships. A dutiful son might have bought his parents a car, or provided for the education of young cousins. But now, living in a different city or even another country, with a greater amount of expendable income, who's to know if he spends that money on a Harley and his latest girlfriend?

Their economic status has for the most part been earned by hard work and smart investments. But underlying assumptions of *karma* (fate) and ascribed respect may keep some middle-class Indians from giving to others the kind of respect they themselves have earned.

The new middle class consists of self-made men and women. But their road to prosperity is not one that most Indians can travel. Although the government has poured money into higher education since Independence, most Indians have not been educated to university entrance level. Thirteen percent of the middle class come from the "backward" and "scheduled" castes that make up 50 percent of India's population, but most people are too poor and too distanced from the education and social networks that lead to decent jobs to rise along with them. In recent decades, quota requirements in education and government have made it possible for some in the "backward" class to begin the economic climb, but ancient hierarchies and ongoing discrimination make the climb a treacherous and difficult one.

Many in the middle class are using their newly found power not only to meet the needs of their extended family, but to care for the poor. Small nonprofit organizations focused on meeting the needs of women and children are springing up all over India. But it may be difficult for the middle class to see itself as a unique "class," since caste and religion are the key defining cultural categories. The lack of a collective identity, or awareness of the strength of their combined resources, may limit the contribution of this new group to the advancement of the Indian economy or society as a whole.

Foreigners and Hierarchy

In India, don't expect to find what Westerners regard as fairness or equality. These are not values that Indians see as necessary or even good.

In the West, we also have hierarchies built on class, personal, and political history, and family-taught prejudices. But for most of us, these demarcations are permeable and can be overcome by effort or changed over time. That is alien to the Indian concept of hierarchy. One's role in the community and family, one's identity, educational, and vocational options, and appropriate life connections are all determined by the caste and family into which one is born.

Respect is considered a fundamental right of those who were born "above." To disrespect (by disobeying or disregarding) someone above you is serious enough to bring shame, disgrace, and social punishment not only on you, but on your family and all those connected to you. For those working or living longer-term in India, it will be important to keep this in mind. If you inadvertently shame a colleague or superior you may find yourself out of favor and unable to get your job done.

This difference in values may cause the visitor to experience a degree of internal, if not external, conflict. But hierarchy can sometimes work to your advantage as a foreigner. Caucasian men are shown respect as someone "above" on the social scale. This is especially true if you are "the boss." White women, too, seem to be in a special category, given access, privilege, and respect often withheld from Indian women.

This does not apply to all foreigners. As in many places in the world, discrimination and sometimes ill-treatment come according to pigmentation. Darker-hued people from anywhere, be it India, Africa, or Europe, will find themselves at the bottom of the social pecking order. People from neighboring countries come up against old prejudices and long-held stereotypes, born of fear of China to the north, or tied to the Tamil–Sinhala conflict in the south. Pakistan and India suffer from more than sixty years of bloodshed, war, and bad attitudes on both sides.

RELIGION

Despite differences in theology, history, and practice, all Indians believe that religion is crucial to one's identity and to the well-being of family and society.

> **Worship without devotion is a waste of leaves [used in rituals].**
> *Telugu proverb*

Hinduism

Eighty percent of Indians are Hindu. Ask ten Hindus to describe their religion, and you may get ten related but not identical answers. Hinduism is a relatively recent formulation of a belief system that developed over millennia. Philosophically, Hinduism is pantheistic monism, essentially the belief that "All is One, One is All, All is God." There is one undifferentiated, impersonal divine consciousness, Brahman, which is the only Reality. Everything else is *Maya*, or illusion.

The purpose of the Hindu sacred texts is to illuminate the truth that All is One, lighting the way to escape the illusory cycle of death and rebirth, returning to the One. Hinduism as it is practiced is a religion of story, not history, focusing not on historical events or people, but on ideology and ritual. Many of its sacred writings tell stories

about *avatars*—gods and goddesses that are manifestations of Brahman's descent from the metaphysical to physical, and the most visible part of Hinduism. Though they are merely mirages of the truth, the worship of these deities is seen by all but the intellectual elite as an essential part of Hinduism.

Hindus of both north and south India tell similar sacred stories. But to outsiders, the names and images of the heroes and villains differ enough to be confusing. When asked about variations in the stories of other regions, most Indians are not bothered enough to explain. The variations and, in fact, the stories themselves are not important. It is the reality behind the stories, and one's devotion to the gods and goddesses, that matters.

Hindu philosophy is complex and a matter of debate for intellectuals; but to most Hindus it is simply a way of life. While Hinduism does not have a single unifying holy text, historical leader, or statement of beliefs, there are clearly recognized core beliefs and practices.

Dharma, or duty, sometimes translated as "truth," calls individuals to fulfill their responsibilities within their families and communities by wholeheartedly doing what they were born to do.

Samsara is the cycle of birth, life, death, and rebirth that is the destiny of every living thing. The traditional Hindu insistence on a vegetarian diet is the logical conclusion of this belief in reincarnation.

Karma, the moral law of cause and effect, determines the status of rebirth. Do your duty and it will be better for you next time. Do good and good will happen to you in the next life. Your eventual escape from rebirth, or *moksha*, is determined by your actions in your present life.

Puja, Prasad, and *tilak* are tangible signs of devotion. Wives and mothers, who are responsible for the spiritual well-being of their husbands and children, perform rituals (*puja*) in the home at the shrine of the family deity, first offering flowers, food, or fire to the god, then *prasad* to their families. *Prasad*, the food offered to the god, is usually *ladoo* (sweet nut and chickpea balls) or some other kind of sweet. Purified by prayers and rituals, this holy food carries a blessing from the deity to anyone who eats it.

Pujas performed day and night by priests in the temples confer blessings, forgiveness, or spiritual power to those who go there with offerings of money or food. Hindu worshipers scoop up blessing from the fire that is offered by the priests, sweeping their hands from the flame to their face or the top of their head. Those who have performed the *puja* mark the forehead of the blessed with ash from the fire or from a powder made of turmeric, saffron, clay, or vermilion. Often the shape of the *tilak* indicates the deity worshiped.

What foreigners often take to be the worship of cows is rather a taboo against killing them. Cows have long been protected for social, religious, and practical reasons: they provide life through their milk; they have a prominent place in the stories of Lord Krishna; and at one point in history they were synonymous with high-caste Brahmins.

Islam

Though Islam was introduced to India by conquest, it has become the faith of more than 13.5 percent of the population. From minarets all over India, Muslims are called to prayer five times a day with the declaration, "There is no god but Allah, and Mohammad is his Prophet." For Muslims, religion guides their lives, beginning with the call to prayer whispered in a baby's ear before he or she is named and ending with recitations from the Koran over the grave.

Founded in Arabia in c. 622, Islam is based on the teachings of the Prophet Muhammad. Allah alone is Creator and Judge. Many Hebrew and Christian prophets are honored in Islam, but Mohammad, the last and best of God's messengers, is regarded as "the Seal of the Prophets."

The goal of Islam, meaning "submission," is to do good and shun evil in order to please Allah (God) and by His mercy enter into Paradise. This commitment is expressed through the Five Pillars.

THE FIVE PILLARS OF ISLAM

Shahada: profession of the faith

Salat: praying five times a day

Zakat: almsgiving to the poor

Sawm: self-purification through fasting during the month of Ramadan (when the revelation was given to Mohammad).

Hajj: undertaking the hajj, the pilgrimage to Mecca, at least once in one's lifetime

Because Islam is strictly monotheistic, idols are anathema. The physical representation of the human form, even as art, is expressly forbidden. The Prophet, though revered, is not worshiped.

The word of God, reavealed to the Prophet Muhammad by the Angel Gabriel, recited by him, and later written down, is recorded in the Koran. At home as well as in the mosque, copies of the Koran are placed on a stand, never on the floor or near anyone's feet. To disrespect it is to disrespect God and His prophet. The Koran has been translated, but for Muslims the true revelation is that given to Mohammed—in Arabic.

Indian Muslims, primarily Sunnis, also have distinct practices that are more Indian than Islamic. Sufis, Muslim mystics, came to India in the fourteenth century, spreading Islam through holy men who blended well into the pattern of Hindu gurus. These *pirs*, or living saints, gathered a following while they lived. After death, stories of their holy lives drew people to their tombs, which soon became places of prayer. As tales were told of miraculous cures, the tombs themselves became holy places. Today there are hundreds of *dargahs,* or "portals," to be found all over India. In passing, they might be mistaken for Hindu or Catholic shrines, were it not for the distinctive dress of the worshipers: streams of white-capped men reaching out to touch the tomb as they pray; clusters of black-robed women tying red threads around iron bars surrounding the holy site, making promises to the *pir* or to Allah if the *pir* will but grant their request.

Christianity

Christianity reached India with Thomas, one of the twelve apostles who followed Jesus. The Mar Thoma Church of Kerala traces its roots directly to Thomas, who landed on the Malabar Coast in 52 CE. Though Christianity has been in India for two thousand years, missionaries have, in the last few centuries, contributed not only to the growth of Christianity in India, but also to the development of education and literacy, and to health and medicine.

Making up 2.4 percent of India's population, Christians live mainly in the south and the northeast; 60 percent are Roman Catholic. The largest Indian Protestant Church, the Church of South India, was created in 1947 when Presbyterians, Congregationalists, Methodists, and Anglicans united. Despite sharing a common creed, Indian Christians are divided by details of doctrine and also by the plague of caste. Whether Baptist or Catholic, Jacobite or Church of North India, all are caste-based communities perpetuated by birth, strong social identity, and strict taboos against marriage outside the community.

Forms of Christian worship are as varied as the peoples who call themselves Christian. Some gather in large buildings with stained-glass windows to sing hymns from books that have been translated from English; others meet in homes and sit on woven mats on the floor, singing *bhajans* (religious songs) to the beat of tambourines.

Buddhism

Though Buddhists are a tiny minority of only 6.5 million adherents, Buddhism originated in India and plays an important role in its history and culture. The founder of Buddhism, Siddhartha Gautama, was born a high-caste Hindu in the hills of Nepal in 563 BCE. Abandoning his comfortable life at the age of twenty-nine, he embarked on a search for meaning first through fasting and asceticism and then through meditation. While traveling through Bihar, in northern India, Siddhartha determined to remain under a tree until he understood the reason for living. It was there that he attained enlightenment and understood the Four Noble Truths.

THE FOUR NOBLE TRUTHS

Suffering is universal.

Suffering is caused by desire.

Suffering can be prevented.

Suffering is overcome when desire is overcome.

Having become "The Awakened One" (Buddha), Siddhartha gathered a band of disciples and created a monastic order that continues today.

There are two primary Buddhist tenets. The law of causation teaches that nothing happens by chance, but is based on *karma*. The law of impermanence teaches that everything changes. Nothing is destroyed, but simply returns in a different form, including the human soul through reincarnation.

The aim of Buddhism is to escape suffering and the cycle of rebirth by overcoming all desire and attaining enlightenment. Buddha's prescribed means of reaching

enlightenment was by the Middle Way, spurning both excess and asceticism, and through the Eightfold Path of right view, thought, speech, action, livelihood, effort, mindfulness, and concentration.

Buddhism is philosophically a religion without a god, but the Buddha has become an object of worship for most of India's six-and-a-half million Buddhists. His statues and shrines can be found all across the subcontinent; the three holiest sites in India are Bodhgaya, Bihar, where he attained enlightenment;

Sarnath, outside Varanasi, Uttar Pradesh, where he preached his first sermon, establishing Buddhism by "setting in motion the wheel of truth"; and Kushinagar, near the Nepalese border, where he died.

Sikhism

Guru Nanak, the founder of Sikhism, was born in 1469 to a high-caste Hindu family. He was inspired by the monotheism of Islam, and drawn to both Hindu and Muslim saints. His preaching of a unification of Hinduism and Islam attracted disciples ("*Sikhs*"). Guru Nanak's teachings, which included Hindu and Muslim holy texts, were eventually written down in the sacred book, Siri Guru Granth Sahib.

It is the presence of the Siri Guru Granth Sahib that, for Sikhs, makes a place holy. Many Sikh homes today have a room or a space set apart for the holy book. This Sikh sacred scripture continued to be developed by later Gurus who contributed to Sikh spiritual and communal life in their own ways.

Guru Arjun, the Fifth Guru, built the Golden Temple at Amritsar. It was from there that he judged civil affairs, establishing a tradition of a religious state. The Tenth Guru, Govind Singh, trained Sikhs in military combat to equip them to defend their faith. Singh, who died in 1708, was the last living Sikh Guru. Having created a collective body of initiates known as the *Khalsa*, or Pure Ones, he declared the end of the succession of human gurus and identified the sacred text as Guru for Sikhs in subsequent generations.

The brotherhood of the *Khalsa* are recognized by the five K's: *Kesh* (uncut hair), *Kangha* (a wooden or ivory comb as a symbol of purity), *Kara* (a steel bracelet as a sign of determination), *Kripan* (a sword to defend the weak), and *Kuchha* (shorts, symbolizing alertness). At initiation, *Khalsa* Sikhs take on a new name: men become *Singh* (Lion) and women become *Kaur* (Princess).

Today 2 percent of Indians are Sikhs, with most living in the Punjab. They have been held together by a common culture, as well as by the core beliefs that God is one and that all men are equal. Rejecting the notions of a priesthood or organized decision-making body, local Sikh communities make decisions together based on the Siri Guru Granth Sahib. Attempts, like the one in early 2010, to create a new sect or detour from historical and communally held doctrines are met with censure by leaders and the broader community.

The Hindu belief in *karma* and reincarnation is part of Sikhism. Many Hindu life-cycle rituals, including cremation and the reading of Hindu scriptures, are part of the life of the Sikh. Because of the syncretistic nature of the religion, intermarriage with Hindus is common.

Sikh temples, or *gurdwaras* ("doorways to the Guru"), can be recognized by the Sikh flag flying overhead. These gathering places are centers for worship, religious education, and community service. Look inside and you'll see rows of men, women, and children eating a meal in huge halls where food is served endlessly. Opposing the Hindu caste system, Guru Nanak set up congregations of followers who shared a communal *langar* (kitchen) and meals, thus breaking down caste barriers.

Jainism

India's five million Jains, living primarily in Maharashtra
and Rajasthan, trace their religion through twenty-four
Jinas ("those who overcome"). The last of the *Jinas*,
Vardhamana, or Mahavira ("The Great Hero"), was born
to a ruling family in Bihar in the sixth century BCE. To find
purification of conscience and the meaning of existence,
Mahavira cast off his riches and began what became an
austere quest for truth. He is said to have foresworn
clothing and shelter, and eventually formed a monastic
order, training others to find purity and enlightenment
through asceticism. After many years, satisfied that he had
fulfilled his purpose, Mahavira fasted until he died.

Karma is the foundation of Jainism. Believing that the
soul is made pure by right conduct, faith, and knowledge,
Jains conquer worldly desire through abstinence and
asceticism, and follow a life of nonviolence (*ahimsa*). So
that they do not inadvertently kill insects while breathing
or walking, Jain monks and serious devotees cover their
nose and mouth with a mask and clear their paths with
small brooms. Inactivity cleanses one of desire and action,
reversing the impact of past action. For the Jain, worship
and other religious ritual is not focused on a Being, but
the recognition of the ability of those in the past to
overcome *karma* and extinguish the self.

"Sky-clad" Jains (*Digambaras*) live as Mahavira lived,
within monasteries and without clothes. The few females
that claim to be *Digambaras* must don robes. This
virtually all-male sect teaches that women cannot be
true monks or attain *moksha* (liberation) until they are
reincarnated as men. "White-clad" Jains (*Deravasi*) wear
white robes and mouth coverings. Both groups are divided
by theological debate.

The holiest Jain shrine, carved in 981 BCE, stands on a
hill outside Bangaluru, Karnataka. Every twelve years Jains
come to anoint this vast statue of Gomateshvara, also

known as *Bhagwan* ("lord" or god) Bahubali, with milk, ghee (clarified butter), and saffron. This giant is believed by Jains to be the first human being ever to attain enlightenment, thus becoming the first *Jina*.

Zoroastrianism

Most of India's 80,000 Zoroastrians live in Mumbai, in Maharashtra, and the rest live in Gujarat, where the first Zoroastrians arrived from Persia in the tenth century.

Zarathustra, or Zoroaster, is thought to have founded this religion in Persia sometime before the sixth century BCE, though new scholarship dates it back to 1200 BCE. Under Cyrus the Great, his teachings became the official state religion of the Persian Empire in the sixth century BCE. Inspired by a vision of the Wise Lord, Ahura Mazda, Zoroaster taught a form of religion that stressed moral choice and personal responsibility. In the cosmic struggle between Good and Evil each individual had to choose between those two opposing forces. Good prevails when human beings follow *Humata* (good thoughts), *Harkta* (good words), and *Huvarshta* (good deeds). The followers of Zoroaster in India are called Parsees. They honor Zend-Avesta as their holy book and represent Ahura Mazda, the omnipresent and invisible God, with fire.

Parsees are few in number, since "true Parsees" are those who are born to two Parsee parents. Parsees have no distinctive dress and few temples. Unlike other religious communities in India, the Parsees leave their dead in "towers of silence" to be eaten by vultures. It is the last and best *Huvarshta*.

Tribal Religions

Eight percent of Indians are tribal (68 million, according to the 1991 census). In the past two hundred years, 25 to 60 percent of people from among India's tribes have turned to Christianity. The rest practice various forms of animism. Though taking on some aspects of Hinduism, most tribal beliefs fall outside the traditional definition of Hinduism. Believing that numerous gods or spirits live among them and control their world, these animists appease hostile spirits with offerings, animal sacrifices, rituals, and witchcraft.

The Santhals of Orissa and Bengal believe in a hierarchy of spirits who dwell in the sacred groves at the edge of every village. The Bhils, one of the largest tribes of western India, make terracotta horses believed to be spirit riders who accompany the dead on their journey to the afterlife. The traditional religion of the Todas, a small shepherding community in the Nilgiri Hills in South India, is based on buffaloes. Devotees worship at dairy temples. The Nagas of northeast India, once a tribe of headhunters, take great care to pass on genealogies and to appease the dead.

Modern-Day Gods and Gurus

You don't have to look far to find living gods and goddesses in India. Belief in the multiplicity of deities and their *avatars*, and the concept of a guru who leads devotees to truth, make Indian culture the perfect breeding ground for religious sects such as those of Maharishi Mahesh Yogi, Bhagwan Rajneesh, Shree Maa, Satya Sai Baba, and Ammachi, which gained large international followings in the late twentieth century, and continue to do so today.

Hundreds of men and women like these continue to be sought after as miracle workers and revered as incarnations of the divine. Some of them claim to be only gurus, pointing the way for those who follow. Others are worshiped as gods by devotees who enthusiastically call others to find joy, healing, and purpose in their presence.

KARMA AND FATE

Karma may be a distinctly Hindu doctrine, but karmic thinking, or fatalism, affects all Indians, who believe that there is a force outside yourself, a universal or divine power, that controls your life.

> **Wherever a sinner goes is hell.**
> *Malayalam proverb*

In a world where your place is decided by birth and by caste, and major life decisions are made by others, "fate" may be a comfort. "It was his fate" is a common spoken conclusion, whether after a tragic accident to a loved one or a financial windfall to a friend.

Karma is the motivation for a person to do good in order to improve his or her life, if not now, then in the future or the next life; but it can also be a cop-out. *Karma* may be blamed for a bad marriage as well as for bad character, and can be used as an excuse for leaving the poor to their "deserved" fate.

FAMILY

The family is one of the most important and evident of all Indian values. Family in India means the extended family. Whether living under the same roof in the family home or scattered around the globe, family is the entire network of people who are related to each other by blood or marriage.

> **If everybody tries together even a**
> **mountain can be moved.**
> *Malayalam proverb*

The extended family maintains and defines social boundaries, ensuring that individuals and single family units stay within the culturally prescribed norms. It is the family that forms identity, where values are passed on and lived out, on whom you depend for life and well-being.

Individuality, autonomy, and independence, highly esteemed values in the West, are antithetical to all that Indians traditionally hold dear. There is no such thing as "my property," "my space," or "my decision." The notion of such boundaries in personal relationships is considered ridiculous by Indians. "I am my family." Individuals who act independently are viewed as selfish and bad. Typically those rebels will be corralled through public ridicule or third-party communication (relative A tells relative B who tells relative C until the news comes back to the culprit).

Relationships and social responsibilities are of prime importance, since no one accomplishes anything on their own. Everything, from mothering and naming your children through passing exams, to choosing a spouse, is done with the help of family. It's not uncommon for businesspeople to take time off work to attend the several-day-long wedding of what we might see as a distant relative or to participate in a religious event. These things are viewed as acceptable responsibilities, and people feel obligated, even if not overjoyed, to participate in them. Active participation in life events from birth to death help to reinforce family identity and belonging, and ensure that just as you are there for others, they will be there for you.

SHAME AND HONOR

When people step outside the boundaries, it is not just the reputation of that individual that is at stake, but the reputation of the family. Honor is an attribute of birth, based on caste and class. Honor can be added to, or diminished, by marriage. But all can be undone by failure to live within the socially prescribed boundaries and cultural values. One bad decision, or one traumatic event beyond your control, and all is lost, never to be regained. This is why the honor (*izzat*) of one's family and community must be upheld at all costs.

> **The reputation lost on a betel nut won't come back though you donate an elephant.**
> *Kannada proverb*

Parents, teachers, relatives, religious and government authorities, and even strangers all know the part they must play in the lives of those around them to hold on to the honor of family, community, and country. Children are taught to align their behavior to communal expectations or face ridicule or physical punishment. Comparison with the example of others is a common means of teaching what "proper behavior" and expected outcomes are. Mistakes, slipups, and failures, whether moral, behavioral, or academic, are punished and hidden from public view. Honor depends on it.

If honor dies, other things die with it. Families are boycotted; parents have difficulty finding suitable marriage partners for their children; business and social connections may be severed. In extreme cases those who have brought shame to a family or been shamed by their children or spouse may threaten—or commit—suicide.

Gender and Honor

Traditional social attitudes toward women are one of India's cultural paradoxes. The *Laws of Manu*, described in

Chapter 1, state that a woman has no existence apart from that of her husband or his family. Yet goddesses are not only worshiped, but are among the most feared of the deities. In the same way, women are placed on a pedestal, revered as pure and feared as powerful. At the same time, they are treated as property—valuable property, but property nonetheless.

Whether pedestal or property, a woman has the power to bring down an entire family. Men are the guardians of family honor, including the honor of their wives, mothers, and sisters. Women, however, bear responsibility not only for their own behavior, but for the behavior of their children and their husband. If any of them are found wanting, she may be blamed for the disgrace that results.

Traditional division of labor in Indian families is one way in which male family members protect their women and so uphold the family honor. This arrangement has payoffs for both parties. A man may take on household responsibilities such as grocery shopping so that his wife or daughters do not have go into the public arena, and are thus protected from abuse, including the all-too-common "eve-teasing" (Indian vernacular for the public sexual harassment of girls and women), thus lessening the likelihood of a tarnished reputation.

In the home, women may add to their honor and that of their family by overseeing household servants. Women of status do not need to clean, cook, or drive—others do it. In the West, machines provide household help, but in India, where nothing is done alone and interdependence meets needs of all kinds within the larger community, a servant means not only prestige for one family, but provision and protection for many people. Though increasing numbers of educated, competent women from all levels of society are working outside the home, cultural pressure to be the traditional wife and mother persists.

A milestone on the road to gender equality took place in March 2010 when the Rajya Sabha, the male-dominated upper house of parliament, voted overwhelmingly to reserve a third of all legislative seats across the country for women. The legislation still has to pass the lower house and be approved by fifteen of India's twenty-eight states.

A foreign woman traveling or living in India will in all likelihood experience the best and the worst of Indian men. Learning a few practical tips (see Chapter 7) can help you avoid unnecessary risks to your person and to your own honor. You would do well to attach yourself to a family, coming under the protection of father and brothers and allowing yourself to be mentored by mother and sisters. It's contrary to many Western values and to some women's sense of self, and it will be frustrating; but it may also be enlightening.

PURITY AND TOLERANCE

Implicit in the concept of honor and shame is the idea of purity. Walking the less than sanitary streets of India, some may find it difficult to believe that purity is a value. But being pure is not about being free of germs. It is about separation from anything or anyone with the power to contaminate honor, morals, caste, or identity.

India is famous for its tolerance. Tolerance has been promoted since the time of Gandhi as an essential part of the process of democratization and secularization, but it is a different kind of tolerance from that promoted in the West. Tolerance is not the acceptance of differences as equally good, right, or valid. It is the acknowledgement that differences must be endured for one's group to survive. In fact, it is not tolerance that is the virtue, but coexistence.

All kinds of people live and work side-by-side in every village and town, but personal distance and social distinctions are maintained by rules and roles that are clear to insiders. For example, family and social taboos on conversion and intermarriage are intended to preserve the purity of the religion and the family bloodline. Indians are proud to note distinctions between their people and all others. Stereotypes help to define boundaries and group identity and values. "We" are like this. "They" are like that. "We" do this. "They" do that. Such simple stereotyping extends to foreigners, too. Movies and TV programs from the West, especially the USA, have created an indelible picture of all Westerners as corrupters of morals, religion, and family. Among younger people, the cultural fabric formed by the notions of social and religious purity are beginning to fray as urbanization, education, and globalization challenge traditional Indian mores.

HOSPITALITY, GENEROSITY, AND RECIPROCITY

The warm greeting between friends when they meet on the road; the welcoming smile at the front door; the offer of *chai* when you enter a shop—all these are signs of the wonderful hospitality that visitors to India will experience.

Deeply rooted in the idea that God accompanies or dwells in people is the belief that to offer hospitality to a stranger is to serve a god. Indians rarely offer anything but their best to those who enter their homes. Unaware of economic circumstances or social expectations, foreign visitors may not appreciate the extent of the generosity or of all that is sacrificed to provide what, for them, may seem ordinary or perhaps even inadequate.

A poor villager may serve an unexpected but important visitor the chicken he had been raising for a special family ceremony. A box of sweets is brought to your home when friends are invited to dinner. A man returning home after living overseas brings extravagant gifts for his parents, uncles and aunts, extended family members, and a host of family friends. A new friend gives a gold necklace to your newborn baby. Sharing resources, whether through the offering of food to a beggar or the giving of a substantial loan to a friend, serves to sustain individuals as well as to affirm the social order.

This tradition of generosity has been shaped by the patron–client structures of the past. The prosperity of the landowner and the survival of the landless were ensured, as landlords loaned money to clients, who then worked the land to repay the debt. In many cases the debts became so overwhelming that they could never be repaid and generations of bonded laborers served generations of landed gentry. This formula of relationships between social unequals for mutual benefit is still at work today in India's villages, businesses, families, and communities.

While Indians understand what goes on behind the scenes, visitors rarely will. In many cases, the subtext for hospitality or generosity is the expectation of reciprocity. A neighbor looks after your property while you're out of town; you take meals to his ailing grandmother in the hospital. A servant has served your family well for years; you help finance her wedding. While there are few occasions in India where gifts are exchanged, Indians keep a mental balance sheet that enables them to offer appropriate gifts and hospitality to the appropriate people at the appropriate time.

In many cultures it is taken for granted that individuals going out with friends pay for themselves—but not in India, where the one who invites pays (see Chapter 4).

INDIAN STRETCHABLE TIME

IST officially stands for "Indian Standard Time." By now its conversion to "Indian Stretchable Time" is a well-worn joke, but not a very funny one for anyone from a time-oriented culture. Hindi has the same word, *kal*, for yesterday and tomorrow. Context makes the difference, and in India it is context, not the clock, that matters. With some exceptions, Indians are event oriented. They are not typically late for work, and Indian trains do not wait for anyone. So it is not the absence of a sense of time, but the priority of people and events over the clock. For Indians, time is never "wasted" on people.

To those from places where efficient use of time and visibly productive work days mean money, respect, and personal satisfaction, it may be difficult to comprehend the value of stretchable time. But there are advantages. Respect is shown by allowing people to complete their conversation or business, rather than rushing on to someone or something else. Bonds are maintained and new alliances are forged while chatting over tea.

Expect everything to take longer than you think. One errand that would take thirty minutes back home may take all morning in India. People may not show up for appointments, and coworkers may take longer than agreed upon to finish a project. Give yourself and others a break by lowering your expectations of what can be accomplished in a day. The best medicine for IST is a lot of patience and a little something on hand to do while you wait. And wait you will—expect it!

Indian Stretchable Time is frustrating for time-oriented people. Even Indians who excuse their tardiness with "IST" and a wry smile aren't happy when they have to wait for others. But all Indians know that IST is a fact of life in India. Don't waste time trying to fight it. The slower pace may be hard to swallow, but it can be medicinal and even enjoyable for those who can adjust their expectations.

> **There's always a ditch in front of someone in a hurry.**
> *Punjabi proverb*

chapter three

CUSTOMS & TRADITIONS

HOLIDAYS

In India there are only three official national holidays—Republic Day (January 26), Independence Day (August 15), and Gandhi's Birthday (October 2)—and a multiplicity of religious and regional observances and festivals. Most holidays are religious. For people from every religion, cycles of fasting and feasting are common. Most holidays vary annually, based on lunar months or astrologically determined dates.

Bank holidays are typically public holidays, with businesses closed for the day. If you intend to do business while in India, you need to find out in advance about coming dates that mean closed government and other offices. Ask, too, about processions that may block traffic.

Holiday Highlights
Republic Day
All India unites on January 26 for Republic Day, the day that India became a sovereign nation. It is a great day to visit New Delhi. Presidential awards are given with all of the proper Indian pomp and ceremony. A spectacular televised parade represents every branch of the military, all the states, and the panorama of Indian subcultures.

Independence Day

The celebration of India's independence from the British Empire in 1947 is a huge event across the country. On August 15 schools and businesses close to attend flag-raising ceremonies and to hear the Prime Minister give a state of the union address. You might see kites, as well as flags, flying as children take advantage of the day off.

Shivaratri

In February, especially in Uttar Pradesh, Hindus may fast during Shivaratri, "the night of Shiva," celebrating his marriage to Parvati.

Holi

Holi, or "burning," is a spring festival. This Hindu celebration of the triumph of good over evil is marked by a bonfire in which an effigy of the evil Holika is burned, but the meaning of the holiday is overshadowed by the madness of "playing colors." Holi is viewed as a day to ignore social restrictions and taboos. Buckets of colored water and brightly hued paint powders are tossed over neighbor and stranger alike. Nowhere else is Holi celebrated as it is in Varanasi, the center of Shiva worship and famous for its legal *bhang* shops. *Bhang*, ground cannabis leaves mixed with milk and spices, is the official drink of Holi, and often finds its way into edible snacks.

Ramadan

During the month of Ramadan Muslims over twelve years of age (except pregnant women and the elderly) are expected to abstain from food and drink during daylight hours, and refrain from sinful or selfish behavior. Muslim-run restaurants will be closed during the day. After sunset, family and friends gather to feast, often into early morning. In some neighborhoods you may find it necessary to refrain from eating, drinking, or smoking in public. Eid ul-Fitr is the finale of this monthlong observance of the revelation of the Koran to Mohammed.

Diwali (Festival of Lights)

Bring earplugs if you plan to sleep during the all-night firecracker-filled festivities that mark the weeklong holiday of Diwali in October. The reasons for celebrating it vary

regionally, but the practices of stringing bright lights and giving sweets and gifts are common throughout the country. Most north Indians celebrate Rama's return with his wife, Sita, to Ayodhya after defeating the demon

Ravana. Many Hindus light the way for Lakshmi, goddess of wealth, to find her way to their home during this time. Jains celebrate the day their founder, Mahavira, attained enlightenment. In Bengal, Kali Puja, the worship of the dark goddess, coincides with this festival.

Festivals and Processions

Some festivals are outside the annual calendar. The world's largest is the Kumbh Mela. This "festival of the nectar pot of immortality" is held every three years in one of four locations in North India: Allahabad, Haridwar, Ujjain, and Nasik. In 2001, more than sixty million devotees converged outside Allahabad for the Maha (great) Kumbh Mela, which occurs every 144 years. By stepping into the place where three rivers—the Ganges, the Yamuna, and the Saraswati (a mythical river)—meet, believers hope to wash away a lifetime of sins.

It seems as though every sacred image, from the elephant-headed Ganesh to the Virgin Mary, is carried through the streets in procession at least once a year. Lifted by devotees or carted through town by ox or, more rarely, elephant, these wooden images, festooned in flowers, paint, and

sometimes clothes, are taken from the place in which they are worshiped to a river for ritual bathing.

Sacred events are relived and retold in art, music, and dance. Mythologies are reenacted in *lilas*, or dramas, by painted children who are paraded through the streets of North India as representations of the gods. Stories are retold in the subtle, graceful movements of classical dancers. Whitewashed street musicians in Tamil Nadu blare horns and beat drums as if in a trance. *Phadas*, folk paintings of western India, honor local heroes by depicting their stories on cloth. The variety and number of celebrations and rituals in India is fascinating.

They can, on the other hand, be frustrating for those on business there. Offices may close or be barely functional during major holidays or local festivals; roads may be blocked by processions and crowds; people may be unavailable or preoccupied. There are ways, however, to use these unavoidable events as opportunities—they can be occasions to build personal and cultural bridges. Indians are generally very hospitable. Ask a business acquaintance if you could join their family during a festival. Take them an appropriate gift (see Chapter 4), and don't talk shop. See what normal life is like for them, and ask questions. More trust can be built up on a day like this than in a hundred business meetings.

Processions and *lilas* are not the only reason for suddenly closed businesses or road congestion. You may encounter a political rally that might erupt into a mob protest, or even a riot. Political temperatures run high, and outsiders cannot always judge when a gathering to hear a candidate's speech will turn into an event that requires police intervention. The best approach (unless you're a reporter) may be to find a rooftop from which to observe, if this is what you want. Better still, make a quick getaway. If you are caught on the street when a crowd is incited to riot, or when the police pull out their *lathis* (sticks), go to the nearest shop and ask to stay there until it's all over.

FAMILY EVENTS

Each community in India has its own rites of passage. Most arise from religious beliefs. Some are caste-specific. All are celebrated in ways that highlight the significance not only for the individual, but for the whole community.

Birth

From the moment a baby takes breath, he or she is connected to a family, to a community, to history, and to the Divine through ritual. Life-cycle rituals are as varied as the people who perform them.

A woman will typically go to her maternal home during the last trimester of pregnancy, and remain there until the baby is a month old. Her own mother will look after her and help with the new baby (and any other small grandchildren who may have accompanied their mother).

The historically high infant mortality rate has shaped traditions surrounding childbirth. A child may not be named until he or she is seen to be strong and healthy, being called a pet name or simply "Baby" up till the age of two.

Names are chosen in various ways, depending on the community. Each caste and culture group has its own naming equation. Hindus may consult astrologers for the most auspicious or lucky name. South Indian Christians may choose an anglicized Western or Biblical name. In Tamil Nadu boys may be given their own name in addition to the name of their father and grandfather. In Kerala names may include a "house," or clan, name, indicating one's ancestral family. In any community, you are just as likely to find children named after an Indian movie star as you are a religious hero or deity.

Marriage

Marriage in India can be both holy sacrament and a social or political alliance. The establishment of a new family and the strengthening of the community is so important that parents work hard to find suitable mates for their children, using the extended family, business and social networks, and their connections to the Divine, whether astrologer, imam, or priest.

Most marriages in India are still "arranged." To those from individualistic cultures the practice may seem unfair and even a form of abuse; but "arranged" does not mean "coerced." It is a system that has worked for millennia and is irrevocably connected to India's social system and values. Though, as India's values change, so do its social customs. Suitability for marriage is based less on personality and more on shared caste, class, education, and social standing. The axiom "you aren't marrying the girl, you're marrying her family" is epitomized in Indian culture.

Traditionally, young people live with and are the responsibility of their parents until they marry. Parents oversee and play a major role in all their life decisions. Children are strongly dissuaded from pursuing a profession deemed inappropriate for the family's social position or for finding a suitable spouse. Good Indian parents will do whatever they view as necessary to give their children the best life possible.

Many young people, especially those living and working in cities or outside the country, do date and fall in love, often keeping this secret because of family expectations and social mores. If the potential mate is from the right background, the couple might ask their parents to "arrange" their marriage. But many a Bollywood movie has been made on the premise of a love story turned to tragedy because of rejection by the family.

Today children of marriageable age and their parents are using the Internet to increase their pool of potential matches. The couple has a chance to interact virtually and to be more involved in the decision while maintaining their personal and family virtue and social traditions.

Religion usually trumps all else in such decisions. To marry outside one's religion is to reject parents, family, and one's very self, and for the same reason conversion to another religion is violently opposed. Both bring loss of honor, opportunity, and relationship for the individual and for the entire family.

Though illegal since 1961, dowry remains a fundamental part of Indian marriage. It can be a way for a woman to share in family wealth in a society which, until recently, did not allow women to inherit. But more often the money and gifts do not belong to the girl, but are given to the boy's parents. A girl's family may buy prestige through an alliance with a more educated or wealthy groom. There is also a darker side to this tradition. Dowry deaths, in which the bride becomes the victim of a "kitchen fire," make headlines every year. Deciding that the dowry was not good enough, the mother-in-law or husband "accidentally" douses her with kerosene and lights a match. But for most Indian couples, dowry is simply one aspect of securing a good lifelong companion.

Child marriage has been illegal in India since 1929, when the British administration determined that twelve was the legal minimum age for marriage. In 1978 this was changed to eighteen for women and twenty-one for men. But for two thousand years Indians from some communities have married off their girl children. Rajputs, the Rajasthani warrior caste, initially gave their young daughters in marriage to prevent their abduction by invaders. Today those who give their children in marriage claim that early marriage protects the girl's purity and prevents unnecessary independence. These days it's predominantly a practice of the poor. Little girls mean little dowry and one less mouth to feed. Because such marriages are not registered with the government, statistics are not definitive. Child marriage is still prevalent in Madhya Pradesh, Uttar Pradesh, Bihar, West Bengal, and especially Rajasthan, where research estimates that over 55 percent of girls are married by the time they are fifteen, and 17 percent before the age of ten.

Marriage ceremonies and rituals vary according to religion, sect, caste, and region. Because of the importance of marriage and the need to prove prestige, families spend a great amount of money on wedding extravaganzas, often going into debt to do so.

Hindu Weddings

In North India you may see a groom dressed like a king, riding on a white horse. Seated with him may be a small boy—a lucky charm guaranteeing a first-born son. Surrounded by a hired band, decked out in red uniforms complete with epaulettes and tasseled fez or turbans, the groom's wedding party dances toward the bride and her waiting family.

The couple may meet for the first time at the wedding venue as the bride's family greets the groom's, marking their foreheads with red powder. The couple exchanges garlands and makes the first of their vows. With ceremonial gifts and ritualized words, the bride, dressed in a red sari, beautifully bejewelled, and with intricate henna decorations on her hands, is handed over to the groom's family, to whom she now belongs. As the couple walks around the sacred fire, symbolizing their life's journey together, the priest recites sacred *mantras* and further vows are made. During the ceremony, the bride and groom literally "tie the knot." Hands tied together with a string, the pair, now "one," is blessed by their family elders and the priest.

As part of the ceremony, the groom applies a vermilion dot to the bride's forehead. From that day forward, married Hindu women typically wear the red dot or mark (*bindi*). The style of *bindi* varies regionally. Non-Hindus and single women may also wear a *bindi*, but for most it has become decorative jewelry. Self-adhesive *bindis* in a huge variety of colors and designs can be seen in shops.

Muslim Weddings

Indian Muslims combine Islamic marriage requirements with Indian tradition. Before the big day, women from both the bride's and the groom's families arrive at her home to participate in festivities that include singing traditional songs and performing rituals that are intended to bring out the bride's beauty. Turmeric paste gives her blushing face a glow, and henna decorations on her hands and feet complement her red sari. A band usually parades before the groom on his way to the ceremony. After the *imam* or *aleem* (priest) preaches a short sermon and recites a few *surahs* (passages) from the Koran, the boy sends a formal proposal to the girl, who must accept for the wedding to take place.

Beside mutual consent, there are no specific religious rites for marriage required in Islam. After agreed upon gifts are given between the families, the marriage contract is signed by the couple, the fathers, and the *imam*.

Islam calls for the groom to give *mehar*—gifts to the bride at the time of the wedding; but in India it is often the practice for a dowry to be given by the girl's family to the boy's. The bride and groom are blessed by their elders and sit down to the wedding feast—though not together.

Traditionally, men and women are seated separately. Only after the marriage feast do the bride and groom see each other for the first time. The groom's sister gives the groom the *thaali* (wedding necklace), which he ties around

the bride's neck. The *thaali*, or *mangalsutra* (for Hindus), was originally a Hindu ritual that is an important sign throughout India of being a married woman. The bride now becomes part of the groom's family, and tearfully says good-bye to her own. As she enters her new home, her mother-in-law holds the Koran over her head.

Christian Weddings

Many of the same customs are seen in Indian Christian weddings. Engagement ceremonies may occur a week or a day prior to the wedding. Brides receive special beauty treatments of sandalwood or turmeric. Church ceremonies are only a part of the multiday celebration attended by hundreds or thousands of guests from both families. Wearing white, the bride is escorted up the aisle by her father. Along with the exchange of rings and flower garlands by bride and groom, during the ceremony the girl receives clothing from her new family, which is worn at the reception. There is also the tying of the *thaali*.

Pilgrimage

Pilgrimages are a normal part of life for Indians, and have also become big business. Foreigners from all over the world come to see or participate in them for their own religious reasons or out of curiosity. While Hindu pilgrimage sites predominate, every religion in India has its parallels, and there are thousands of holy sites. Moving away from daily routine to a place full of spiritual meaning and power, pilgrims seek access to and favor from their chosen gods.

Kashi (Varanasi, or Banaras) is to Hindus what Mecca is to Muslims. Every day millions of devotees travel there.

Many intend to spend their last days there, believing that to die and be cremated inside the city limits is to gain salvation.

A forty-one-day period of penance is part of a pilgrimage to Ayyappa, Kerala, 4,000 feet (1,219 m) above sea level in the Western Ghats. Devotees abstain from meat, alcohol, and sex before climbing the mountain, chanting "*Samiye Saranam Ayyappa*" ("O, Lord Ayyappa, I come to thee for refuge"). Not everyone may enter the temple. No woman of childbearing age is allowed, and no one with recently cut hair or shaved face may climb the eighteen steps up to it. In special backpacks, pilgrims carry articles for doing *puja* to Ayyappan, specific food to enable them to make the long trek, and a small blanket. Don't expect to find seats in a bus to the nearby city of Thiruvananthapuram during the Ayyappa festival in March.

For nine days in September, tens of thousands of pilgrims move toward Tirupati, Andhra Pradesh, to the shrine of Sri Venkateswara, Lord of Seven Hills. Standing for hours, pilgrims line up just to catch a glimpse of the deity and to rub camphor or present recently shorn hair as an offering. Daily rituals, which include waking the god and putting him to sleep, can be made in the name of a devotee—for a price. The temple of Tirupati Tirumala Balaji is one of the wealthiest religious sites in the world, second only to the Roman Catholic Vatican.

The "Lourdes of the East" is found in Velankanni, in Tamil Nadu. During a ten-day festival in September Catholics and many others come to this most popular of all Indian shrines looking for miracles. Since the sixteenth century people have reported appearances of Our Lady of Velankanni asking for milk for her baby boy, curing the lame, and requesting a chapel to be built in her name. Because of the hundreds of healings that have taken place there, this manifestation of the Virgin is called *Arokia Matha*, or Mother of Good Health.

A BLESSING FROM THE GODS

No Hindu celebration is complete without *prasad*— food that has been offered to a deity. If you are offered *prasad*, typically a sweet, it is proper to take it with your right hand and immediately put it into your mouth. It is believed to be infused with the power or blessing of the god to whom it was offered. Indians of other faiths will probably not be offered it out of respect for their religion. You don't need to eat it if it is contrary to your own convictions. Refusing *prasad*, if done with humility and respect for those offering it, will not offend anyone. You will be respected for holding to your own form of devotion.

Death

Someone in India dies every six seconds. With nearly fifteen thousand funerals daily, rituals surrounding death are a common sight.

Hindu Rituals

Bathed, clothed, and covered with flowers, a body is carried to the cremation grounds. While infants and small children may be buried or enshrouded and set adrift on a holy river, Hindus typically cremate their dead.

Women grieve at home. Only male relatives and friends gather around the funeral pyre, while priests perform the last rites and the eldest son lights the fire that will release the spirit of the deceased to be reborn. When the attending priests have made sure the body is burned and the proper rituals are complete, the bone fragments and ashes are gathered and scattered on a river.

The family remains ritually "polluted" for a number of days, unable to perform *puja* at the family shrine, participate in religious events, or visit the homes of others. Pictures of the deceased are displayed in the home and adorned with garlands, and small plates of food are offered to the spirit of the loved one. Memorials take place during the first week, on the thirty-first day, and on the first anniversary. It is disrespectful for anyone to marry during the year after the death of an immediate family member.

Widows traditionally dressed in white and could not remarry. In the past, and even in some remote areas today, a Hindu widow, tied to her husband in this life and the next, would throw herself on to his funeral pyre.

Muslim Rituals

Muslims believe in prompt burial following a ritual cleansing of the body. Like Hindu women, Muslim women are not allowed at funerals. Male relatives lift the bier, carrying the carefully wrapped body to the burial ground. The deceased is placed in the ground facing toward the Ka'bah in Mecca, ready for the resurrection on the Day of Judgment. Male mourners throw earth into the grave as they recite a verse from the Koran. Tombstones should not be near the grave. Feasts of remembrance are held on the fortieth day, at four, six, and nine months, and on the first anniversary.

Christian Rituals

Family comes from near and far to mourn, or to comfort those who mourn, the loss of a loved one. The body is carried to the church cemetery in a coffin, or sometimes on a palanquin, accompanied by family and community, and a priest or pastor performs a traditional Christian funeral. The family will visit the cemetery on Christian holidays and other important occasions. As with other religions in India, Christians mark death anniversaries and refrain from arranging marriages during the one-year mourning period.

SUPERSTITIONS AND OMENS

No one likes to be thought of as "superstitious." One person's superstitions are another's beliefs. India, full of people of faith, is also filled with a vast store of what outsiders might consider superstitions and belief in omens that shape daily life and foretell future events. While many of these arise from religious stories, most are commonly held across religious, caste, and subcultural lines.

Many beliefs and practices are related to the fear of being cursed. People of every class and caste have practices that are believed to protect from the evil that might fall on them through the jealousy, ill wishes, and verbal curses of others.

Some Common Beliefs

- To see a crow fly over your house is a bad omen. A crow cawing signals the arrival of guests. Whether that's bad or good luck may depend on the guest! Seeing a peacock is lucky. Hearing a peacock is unlucky. An owl is a warning to prepare for tragedy.

- A dream of marriage is lucky. A dream of death is unlucky. Dreams have meanings, and should be paid attention to, especially if you dream of a departed ancestor coming to you with a message.
- Itching eyes may indicate that someone is jealous of you and is planning your demise. Jealousy is a constant worry in India and special precautions are taken to protect oneself from this dangerous destroyer. Amulets and charms worn on a wrist, the hand of Fatima painted on a wall, or fasting prayer and special offerings are believed to ward off the "evil eye."
- Days of the week and specific dates matter when planning marriages, long-distance travel, or new construction. Hindus will consult an astrologer before making any important plans.
- At home, the direction you lay your head in bed can determine your future happiness. *Tulsi* (basil) trees outside your door bring good fortune. In south India, especially in the villages, women clean the front porch or entry in the early morning, pouring rice or rice powder into intricate patterns to protect the home from evil spirits and to welcome blessing.
- A bride must step into her husband's home for the first time with her right foot, or misfortune will strike. Brides themselves are auspicious, bringing good luck to those who set eyes on one.
- If you are lucky enough to be invited to a wedding, be sure you do not give knives (which "cut" relationships) or cut flowers (dead items, fit for the dead). Cash is always safe, but must be given in odd numbers. You will surprise the couple (or their parents) by giving it in the culturally appropriate way: single bills. (It's best if you give US dollars or British pounds sterling.)

CLOTHES MAKE THE MAN (AND WOMAN)

Most men in India wear Western-style shirts and trousers. During the time of the Independence Movement, Gandhi made *kadhi*, handwoven cotton, popular. Today the *kadhi kurta* (Indian-style shirt) is still the choice for politicians and can be found in tourist shops. It is often worn with a *dhoti*, a white rectangular cloth wrapped to form loose pants. The *dhoti* used to be worn daily, and still is in many villages and in places in Rajasthan, but over most of India today it is worn only for special occasions. In the south, *lungis*, patterned cotton sarongs, may be worn by men at home and by some workers in public.

Elegant and colorful saris and practical *shalwar kameez*—long trousers and a long tunic top—are still the typical dress for women. Other women's wear varies regionally and is often based on age or life stage. Young women today often wear jeans with an Indian-style top.

India can be hot—very hot. But if you are there on business or want to be treated with respect (especially as a woman) don't wear shorts or tank tops. Women can beat the heat and look elegant at the same time by learning to tie a sari or, more simply, wearing a *shalwar kameez* that can be bought ready-made or skillfully tailored in a day.

Though you can't tell it from Hindi films, modesty is important. Women should not show too much skin, even when wearing a sari. The *dupatta* (scarf) and the *pallu* (end of the sari) are traditionally used to cover head, shoulders, breasts, and midriff from male view. Even modestly dressed women may be accused of using their eyes to seduce men. To avoid miscommunicating when in public, women should not look men in the eye, or intentionally touch a man. Humility and even invisibility allow a woman to bear the "good" label in Indian society.

MAKING FRIENDS

FRIENDSHIP

Friendship for Indians does not mean a casual acquaintance; it means a lifelong attachment. Childhood friends, school classmates, and college roommates provide companionship, a sense of place, and relational and vocational opportunity throughout one's lifetime.

Indians tend to be affectionate and expressive, with a deep sense of loyalty and belonging. People go out of their way to meet their friends' needs and to be present and actively helpful during crises and trouble. Many are even willing to risk life and livelihood for one another. If an Indian considers you a friend, you have entered into a relationship—and a network of relationships—that will bring joy and also responsibility, for friendship brings with it expectations that are not always anticipated by Westerners. (See Chapter 2, Generosity, Hospitality and Reciprocity.)

In individualistic or work-focused societies, we may call a friend after several weeks, or even months, and expect to pick up where we left off. In India, prolonged silence or absence of spontaneous visits can result in hurt feelings and damaged relationships: friends are "family," and require a higher degree of commitment.

Foreigners and Friendship

It's not difficult to strike up an acquaintance in India. Indians are curious about foreign visitors and more than willing to enter into conversation. Shopkeepers offer *chai* (tea) or a "cold drink" as you step in from the heat. People on the street offer help when you look lost. Fellow train passengers will gladly share their food (warning you with a smile that "it might be too spicy for you!") Students and others will want to practice their English. The extensive use of English initially makes finding friends easier. If you are willing to learn their language, that's even better.

Indian body language, social cues, and assumptions differ so greatly from those in the West that it may be difficult for someone just entering the country to discern who has the potential for becoming a true friend, and who is befriending you merely for personal gain. This is a constant source of tension for Americans and Europeans, who may be seen as having the power to help people into affluence and opportunity, whether through networks, gifts of cash, or even marriage. It's especially tricky as true friends are expected to share resources and offer assistance and support, financially and socially as well as emotionally. A not-so-subtle indication of a financial need or a direct request for a business connection is perfectly acceptable among friends. So how do you know who your friends are? You will discover them when you are in need. Your Indian friends will be there for you in ways that may surprise and humble you.

MAKING CONVERSATION
Getting Started

Greeting in India is a matter of both showing and receiving respect. But how can you respectfully greet people in a country with twenty-two official languages and a seemingly infinite number of subcultures? Don't worry. It's probably apparent at first glance that you are a visitor, and no one will expect you to know all their ways. Surprise them! Learn a few helpful phrases (see Chapter 9) and observe how Indians of your age and gender greet others.

Whether in English or with your newly acquired local phrases, introduce yourself to people in the neighborhood. Ask to accompany your host or a new friend to the market or on an errand, or invite them to go with you somewhere. Drop in on a colleague, saying you'd like their help to understand your new surroundings.

Topics of Conversation

Everywhere you go in India, people will ask you the same questions: What's your name? Where are you from? How long have you been here? What are you doing? When are you going home? (For those staying longer-term, the last question may feel offensive. But don't take it personally. It probably comes from the perspective that one's primary place is with one's family and community.) Have ready a brief description of yourself and your family, especially if you are living in India. You may want to cover the essentials without giving away information you—or they—feel is inappropriate. For example, many Indians are not shy to ask about money issues, including your income. If questions about your finances embarrass you, be prepared with an ambiguous answer.

Many topics viewed as personal are fair game in India. Indians do not hesitate to talk politics. They will ask your opinion of your own country's policies (of which they are well aware) as well as of India's politics and world issues. They will comment on child-rearing practices, attire (especially if a foreign woman is wearing a sari or *shalwar kameez*), and appearance. They will freely share information about their children's academic successes, and will want to hear about your own children's education and aptitudes. If you are single and over twenty-five, they will ask you why you're not married, and will advise you on finding a suitable spouse. If you are a woman planning to live in India for any length of time, prepare for questions about your whole family and why you've abandoned them. Although many Indian men live abroad for educational or financial reasons, it's less common for single or unaccompanied Indian women. Your reasons may not make sense to your new friends. Don't expend too much energy trying to help people understand you. They can't. But they can still learn to love and trust you over time.

Taboos

Indians generally do not discuss sexual matters, including dating, boyfriends or girlfriends, marital or family problems, or children's misbehavior or poor academic performance. If an Indian asks questions on these topics or offers unsolicited information about his or her sex life or marriage problems, you can be sure that this is not culturally acceptable. It is time to end the conversation. Because of the diversity of beliefs in India, religion may be avoided as a topic of conversation in a social setting.

Yes and No

Like much of Indian culture, the use of "yes" and "no" may confuse and confound visitors. But Indians understand exactly what is being said.

"Yes" is a cord that ties people together. Indians will say "yes" to maintain a relationship and their honor. It's shameful to refuse a request or to be ignorant of a helpful answer. In general, Indians will drop whatever they are doing to meet the needs of family, community, or guest, and whether you're asking if they know the way to the station or if they can take you there, you will usually hear a "yes." Make sure, if the information or instruction is important, to ask more than one person. Indians do it all the time. They know what "yes" means.

One important phrase you need to know is "I will try." If you invite someone to an event or a party, or have asked for some specific help, and they respond, "I will try," they have just declined. They value your friendship, and don't want to risk offending you with a straight refusal. So expect them to be absent or unavailable. When you can't accept an invitation or give help to a friend, don't say, "Sorry I can't." Say, "I will try." They'll understand.

"No" will be the answer to your offer to help or serve them. The key is to ask three times. If, after the third offer, your friend still says "no," it's a true no. You will be considered polite if you do the same. When offered food the first time, politely decline. In all likelihood you will be asked again. If so, simply say "yes, thank you." If not, it means they're used to Westerners. Next time with that friend you'll know to say "yes" the first time!

Which "No" Is It?

She had recently arrived in the USA from India and I invited her to my home for dinner. Offered a second helping of food, she responded politely, "No thank you." "Is that an Indian no or an American no?" I asked. She replied, "An Indian no." Laughing with her, I spooned more food on to her plate.

Personal Space

You may find a great disparity between your sense of personal space and the close proximity of both friend and stranger. If you don't look Indian, be prepared to be stared at everywhere outside the major cities. Curious folk may summon up the courage to touch the hair of a fair-haired girl. If you are carrying a baby around, you'll find yourself warding off the inevitable pinching of the baby's cheeks.

There is a lot of hand-holding in India, but not across gender. Men may hold hands as they walk down the street. Boys of all ages drape their arms around each other. Girls and women often greet one another with a kiss on the cheek, and clasp hands as they share stories. These are all signs of affection and friendship, and should not be mistaken for sexual behavior.

As a visitor to India it is never appropriate to hold hands with, put your arm around, or express affection, physically or verbally, to someone of the opposite sex. This is true in public even with your spouse. Handshaking is a common and usually acceptable greeting when you're in a city, but not always. If you are introduced to a woman, wait for her to extend her hand first. (For more details on appropriate greetings, see Chapter 9.)

GIVING
Who Pays?
In India, whether you invite someone for a cup of coffee or an expensive banquet, you are expected to pay the bill. Don't be caught unawares by this, and expect others to pay their share. They won't. If a friend invites you, you can expect him or her to insist on paying. Feel free to argue, or simply make sure that you extend the invitation next time.

Gift Giving
Everyone loves gifts, but in India they are an important aspect of establishing and maintaining relationships. Twenty-four-carat gold jewelry, electronics, and other expensive gifts are given by family and close friends to newborns and newlyweds, and on special occasions.

Because of the need to maintain equilibrium in relationships through reciprocity, expensive gifts from a visiting friend or business partner may produce a sense of obligation and stress that will create a barrier to the relationship in the future. As a visitor or foreign guest, you should not feel compelled to compete with gifts given by Indians to Indians.

If you receive an expensive gift, or hospitality is lavished on you in a way that feels excessive, do not feel obliged to return in kind. Keep gifts simple and meaningful. A box of sweets, a basket of fruit, or a specialty from your own country is a thoughtful gift when visiting a friend for the first time. If you bring chocolate from home, make sure you carry it in your hand luggage and give it to people you meet at the beginning of your journey. Chocolate sold in India has a higher wax content to keep it stable in high temperatures.

Small toys or an English book will make children smile. Anything that shows where you come from—a calendar with photos, for example—will be valued by your new friends. Other welcome gifts might be brand-name cosmetics and perfumes, moderately priced pens, music CDs, DVDs, or T-shirts from a local university or sports team. If you are on a smaller budget, candy bars, hot chocolate packets, barrettes, or postcards from home are perfectly acceptable.

Most Indians, whether Hindu or Muslim, do not drink alcohol, so make sure that it is acceptable before giving wine or spirits. Leather may not be appropriate either, for religious reasons. A man should not give jewelry or flowers to a woman, as it is considered too personal; and cut flowers are not generally valued as a gift.

If you didn't bring gifts from home you'll need help to find culturally appropriate local gifts. The things you find beautiful in India are not always prized by Indians. A basket of fruit is appreciated when visiting a home, and cash inside a greeting card is good for special occasions. Better still, ask friends and acquaintances for suggestions.

When Giving Is Not Friendship

Beggars will greet you everywhere. If you are in India to stay, you will have time to understand the system and to make decisions regarding how to respond to them and the soul-piercing poverty visible at every turn. Don't be duped by the wide eyes of a child, the bandaged hands of a leper, or your own emotions. If you give them money it will go to others, may not benefit them at all, and will help to perpetuate the cycle of poverty into which these people were born. If you would like to help the millions who have been reduced to begging by profession, disease, or enslavement, there are many excellent agencies, Indian and otherwise, that could use your money to do lasting good.

VISITING AN INDIAN HOME
Hospitality

People you've just met may invite you home for tea, dinner, or even for a short stay. To show appreciation for their hospitality, take a small gift, such as a box of sweets. You will be warmly greeted at the door and shown where to put your shoes, which should be taken off before entering. Slippers are not typically provided. Shoes are considered unclean, so no good host would offer a guest footwear worn by others.

There is a proper protocol to an evening in an Indian home. No matter what time you enter a home, with or without an invitation, you will immediately be offered *chai* (tea with milk, sugar, and sometimes spices), coffee (with milk and sugar), water, juice, or sherbet (a popular fruit- or flower-flavored drink.) It is impolite to refuse.

In India, people converse first, eat later. Once the meal is over, everyone knows it's time to go home. People may sit and chat for hours while a foreign guest, possibly used to eating first and conversing after the meal, or having extended conversations over a multicourse meal, may wonder why dinner is not being served. Dinner can happen at any time in the evening. Even families with small children will eat late, waking a child who's fallen asleep on the couch so they can have a little food and a glass of milk before going to bed.

Indians in cities and towns typically eat at a table. In villages, in a poorer home, or at an event with many guests, people may be seated on mats. The women of the house will have spent all day preparing food for an invited guest. Guests may be served the meal alone or with the head of the household. This is a sign of honor. In homes where food may be scarce, it also ensures that guests eat as much as they want without the family being shamed by running out of food. Dessert is not always served at the end of a meal. You will know it's over when the family members get up to wash their hands. Then it's time to thank the hosts for a wonderful meal, say good-bye to everyone present, and go home. You won't be left until you are outside the gate, down the street, or in a car or taxi. It's a sign of connection and protection that is an integral part of all Indian relationships.

Table Manners

You will be offered aromatic foods with copious amounts of rice or perfectly round handmade chapattis until you either leave a small amount of food on your plate or refuse by putting your right hand over your plate. When offered the first time, it's polite to decline. You will be asked again.

Indian food tastes better when eaten with one's fingers. Use your right hand. If you haven't already mastered the technique, ask your host to teach you.

There is always provision for washing your hands before and after a meal. Many Indian dining rooms are fitted with a basin for this purpose. Generally, food should touch only your fingertips, up to the first knuckle. Though people will be polite if you dirty your whole fingers or the palm of your hand, they will be disgusted. If you feel too uncomfortable or make too much of a mess eating with your fingers, feel free to ask for a spoon.

During a meal, it's acceptable to use your left hand to serve yourself or others, but you probably won't have to. The women of the household will be standing at the ready to serve. In fact, it is not polite to reach for food, and you should never have to ask. It will be offered. If it's not offered, it may be an indication that demand exceeds supply. So take your cue from your Indian hosts. You can tear chapattis, nan, or parathas using two hands. Outside close family, it is never polite to touch someone else's food or eat off another's plate, and never drink out of someone else's glass.

Observing these few points of etiquette will make your visit more enjoyable for you and your hosts. But regardless of your manners or mistakes, you can be sure that all your needs will be met with the greatest possible care and generosity. Besides food and drink, you may well be offered a place to stay, connections in other parts of India, and a ride or an escort to your next destination. It's a matter of friendship for your host to extend every resource for your benefit. They are bound to treat you, their guest, as they've been taught to do in every Indian home and all of India's legends—as a god.

PRIVATE & FAMILY LIFE

NOT SO PRIVATE
Looking Without Seeing
You may find the word "private" in Indian language dictionaries. You will not, however, find much privacy in India—or not in ways you recognize. Westerners define privacy in terms of personal space, confidential information, and freedom from intrusion. But in India, in general, privacy is not about what's hidden, but about what's ignored.

Indians develop the skill of looking without seeing early on. In many rural areas, fields double as toilets. In towns, teenage boys in *lungis* or shorts can be found soaping up at the public water pump. In the river, women discreetly wash and change. Large numbers of people share small spaces: an extended family lives in a tiny two-room hut; a couple and their children share a bedroom in an urban apartment. In spite of obvious deterrents to intimacy, eighteen million babies are born in India each year. Privacy is maintained as people avert their eyes or ignore the activity.

Looking without seeing is difficult for a visitor who is bombarded by new and fascinating sights; but out of respect for the privacy of those around you, learn to ignore them, or look, if you must, out of the corner of your eye.

In an Indian family home there's no such thing as personal space. You may drop in on a friend to find them and their family or friends comfortably gathered on a bed for a chat or a nap. Bedrooms are considered common space, and people don't usually knock before entering. Even hotel staff may give only a cursory rap on the door as they open it. If privacy matters to you, you will need to lock doors. Saying "Please wait here. I'll be right back" may work, but only some will take the hint. Some may tag along to keep you company.

Bathrooms are the exception. You will get some privacy there, though on a rare occasion even a woman will find a public toilet has no stall doors.

Possessions, too, are not "mine," but "ours." Family and close friends may borrow all kinds of things from one another, including money, often without seeing the necessity of returning it. It's not theft or thoughtlessness. It's communal property.

Photo Op?
If you were at the other end of your camera, would you want your picture taken in that situation? If not, think twice before you take the photograph.

Family Secrets
Indians do keep some things private, hidden even from close friends and extended family. Mental illness, depression, and sexual and physical abuse are discussed fairly openly in many Western societies. In India such things as Grandma's schizophrenia, Dad's drunken rages, a cousin's mentally retarded child, Auntie's divorce, or the rape of a sister are intensely guarded secrets that must not be exposed. Family reputation, social status, and the marriageability of daughters are at stake.

You may feel no qualms about relaying your own family's mental health history or personal or even general cultural stories of abuse or divorce, but Indian taboos on these topics will ensure that if you choose to share those "private" matters, respect and trust will be lost. Your work relationships may become strained, and friends may suddenly seem to be uncomfortable around you.

THE FAMILY HOME
Contrasts and Conveniences

Flying into any major airport in India, you will get a glimpse of the many kinds of places people call "home." Delhi's and Kolkata's high-rise blocks; Mumbai's and Chennai's masses of shingle-roofed lean-tos and ramshackle dwellings; Kerala's whitewashed houses surrounded by lush tropical gardens; the blue and pink rooftop terraces of Rajasthan.

On the train you will pass some of India's 500,000 villages. Thatched roofs atop bright blue plastered dwellings, small clusters of homes with red-tiled roofs, and wooden huts on stilts above green paddy fields house the 75 percent of India's rural population.

In every town and city you're confronted with the uncomfortable juxtaposition of rich and poor. Slums visible from the villas of the wealthy; day laborers from city outskirts sleeping on sidewalks outside the apartment complexes they're building to shelter middle-class families; homeless families doing the best they can with a piece of plastic and a few scrounged bits of metal or wood.

Though "home" can be a single room in a multifamily dwelling or a multistoried marble mansion, for most, the family home is not very different from one in any other part of the world: a a place to sleep, sit, and cook. Wooden or woven platforms called *chaarpaai* provide seating for many people, but middle-class homes have living rooms complete with couches, chairs, and, in the cities, TVs. Bedrooms are typically shared. It's not uncommon for a mother and her children to sleep together in the same bed. Kitchens are functional spaces filled with steel or brass pots. Sometimes there is an outside kitchen, where the women or servants prepare the more labor-intensive dishes or foods, like fish, that might create unpleasant odors indoors. You may find a refrigerator in the dining room, along with a porcelain basin for washing before and after meals. Many Indian homes have a space set apart for worship or prayer. Hindus may have a small shrine where women perform daily rituals for the well-being of their families.

Middle-class homes have bathrooms and toilets. If there's no shower, there will be a bucket and a cup; guests are generally expected to bring their own toiletries and towels. The toilet may be separate. Indians do not generally use toilet paper; instead you will find water and a cup. If you do find paper, it's usually disposed of in a waste receptacle, rather than flushed after use.

A Day in the Life

Most women in India are up before sunrise to get ready for the day. Usually with the help of servants or other women in the home, they prepare breakfast and perform the necessary daily religious rituals before waking the men and children. After breakfast everyone gets to their work, whether outside or inside the home.

For the majority of Indians, daily work is focused on meeting daily needs. Only 50 percent of India's children attend school. Those who don't are expected to help at home or, when old enough, work to help support the family.

The laundry man or woman comes by the house each week to deliver cleaned and pressed laundry, and to collect more washing. An ironing trolley may be found at the end of the block for pressing needs. All manner of household goods can be bought right outside the home, from milk and eggs to brooms and dustbins.

Meal preparation is a full-time occupation for many women. For those without the luxury of refrigeration, groceries must be purchased daily. Supermarkets have sprung up in urban India, but most people still shop in local markets or family-owned stores. The butcher or the fishmonger knows his customers and what they usually buy. Credit is extended, to be repaid on a stated date. Stopping by the vegetable stall, an Indian woman orders what she needs, knowing the grocer's son will deliver it in time to prepare the evening meal.

People eat two to four times a day, depending on income, occupation, and lifestyle. Lunch is the main meal. Public schools may provide children with a lunch of rice and *dhal* (lentils). Most schoolchildren, and their working parents, carry a *tiffin* (steel lunchbox, or stacked set of boxes) holding freshly cooked food from home. "Tea" in the early evening can be anything from *chai* (tea) to *tiffin* (in this case, a light supper or heavy snack).

Teatime is visiting time. Friends, business colleagues, or family from across town will drop in to chat. Families sit down to their evening meal between 8:00 and 11:00 p.m.

Extended family expectations and needs, children's school and tutoring, two working parents, frequent guests and drop-in visitors, traffic and transportation chaos, and long commutes in the city all contribute to the stress of daily life. But in this interdependent society, networks of mutually beneficial relationships ease the strain.

Most women do not have to manage household responsibilities alone. Extended family nearby, or even in the same house, means that mothers-in-law, sisters, aunts, and cousins help with food preparation, child care, and other aspects of daily home management.

Traditional caste and class divisions of labor and continued low levels of education, especially for women, contribute to the widespread practice of keeping servants. Both day and living-in servants help with chores in the home, drive children to school, run errands, and serve as security guards at night. Wages are low, but include food and, for resident servants, a roof over their heads. Abuse of all kinds does, of course, happen. But for many these arrangements provide sustenance and practical help for today as well as accessibility to the service and resources of an even larger network.

Family Structures
As a traditional culture, the husband and father is considered the head of the Indian home. When multiple generations live in the same house, the eldest male is king. The wife and mother, however, also has a powerful place in the hierarchy.

The primary relationship is between the mother and her first-born son. Her place in the family is elevated by the birth of a son who becomes, in effect, her retirement plan. The eldest son traditionally bears the responsibility to care for his parents, financially and physically, in their old age. Who he marries matters not only for him, but also for his parents and unmarried sisters.

India has boasted one of the lowest divorce rates on the planet—around 1 percent. But over the past twenty years, divorce in the cities has rocketed to 7 percent. This rapid increase is an indicator of a drastic culture shift taking place that is affecting Indian family life. Isolation from extended family, financial independence for women, career and time pressures for double income couples, greater education and understanding of legal rights, and media-spawned changes in marital expectations are redefining not only marriage but also identity among younger generations.

Women's Work

The strength of Indian women is seen in every family, whether she is a wife caring for home and family, a corporate CEO managing hundreds of employees, or a laundress beating clothes by the river. Since the opening up of the Indian economy in the 1990s, the number of women working in government and the private sector has doubled. Women are becoming financial contributors to family wealth and status. The increase in education and vocational opportunity may slowly change how women are viewed in families and in society.

Women comprise 25 percent of the formal workforce. Considered physically and intellectually weaker than men, women in employment are paid less than their male counterparts, and their work at home is taken for granted. And, tragically, as the number of women in the marketplace has climbed, so has violence against women. Rape, kidnap, torture, and beatings have all risen sharply in the past decade. It's estimated that 90 percent of all working women in India are not counted among "working women." They labor in fields, in construction, and as domestic servants for little or no pay. Even when a young woman receives a good education and income, these are still primarily viewed as assets for the marriage market. Starting a business, developing a career, or taking on upper-level management responsibilities remains difficult for women who, in general, are still held fully responsible for running the home and family.

CHILDREN
Bringing Up Baby

Though every family is different, Indian parents have common values. They willingly make sacrifices for the good of their children, even if it means the father has to work in a distant city or country to earn enough for proper education or the mother goes without adequate food to see her children well nourished.

A close bond is created between mother and child by constant physical contact throughout infancy and childhood. Children share the mother's bed, may receive a daily oil massage, and may be breastfed until two or three years of age. When old enough to eat solid food, the child is fed from the mother's hand. Even when children are older, mothers make sure that on special occasions, such as a birthday, cake and other special foods come from her hand.

Sweets are often used to keep babies and children from fussing. Many common practices used to keep babies happy appear overindulgent to Western eyes. But these actions not only stop tears and tantrums, they develop a deep sense of interdependence, in contrast to Western parenting, which has traditionally been geared to develop independence and autonomy.

Indian children are never alone, even when they sleep, and the common Western practice of teaching an infant to sleep in a separate room may be seen as abuse by good Indian parents. Infants and toddlers are carried throughout the day by mother, aunts, older siblings, or servants. Children of all ages are expected to play together and to look after each other. It's from older siblings, cousins, and neighbors that younger children learn the rules of social order and the respect for hierarchy.

Boys learn early that they have a special place in the order of things. Mothers jealously guard their relationship with sons not only while they are children, but into adulthood. While girls learn how to take care of home and family, boys are usually exempt from chores and are given little responsibility, except for doing well in school. Boys are spiritually safeguarded, as well: in some parts of India male infants and toddlers may be dressed as girls or have a black dot drawn on their cheek with kohl to ward off jealousy and the evil eye.

Whether male or female, middle class or villager, social expectations shape and supersede personal aspirations and desires as children grow into adulthood. Despite this, there is a deep strain of romance evident among teenagers and single young adults. Crushes on the opposite sex, tinged with Bollywood-style fantasies about falling in love, are prevalent.

Boys and girls (as they are called through college) may be segregated in school and social settings as they grow older to prevent inappropriate emotional entanglements or sexual misconduct. Romantic love is equated with sexual activity. Because most marriages in India are still arranged, even the suspicion of improper conduct can bring tragedy or ruin, especially for the girl, for the sisters of both parties, and for the reputation of the extended families. Parents help teenagers, by any means necessary, to focus their energies on education, to work for the benefit of the family, and to uphold the respect of the family name.

Education

Learning institutions have existed in India for millennia.

Today 700,000 primary schools, 110,000 secondary schools, 17,000 colleges, 900 polytechnics, 217 state universities, 20 central universities, and innumerable private institutions of all kinds offer education to the next generation. Though the number of higher institutions and the number of students in higher education continue to rise, still only one in 14,000 Indians goes to university.

India's children have a constitutional right to free education to the age of fourteen, which is compulsory. For decades the government has instituted programs to promote education for all. In the past ten years illiteracy rates have dropped and more girls are registering for, and remaining in, school. In an effort to give greater opportunity for social uplift to underprivileged communities, the law now requires a certain number of places in tertiary institutions to be reserved for "scheduled castes and tribes." But according to the 2009 UNESCO report on education, India is the most illiterate country in the world. Caste, class, and gender distinctions continue to be reinforced by the educational system.

Middle- and upper-class families can afford the best available private education. In south India, 10 percent attend parochial and private schools, where the education is often in English. In the north, private education is increasingly preferred, even by the poor; but because private schools do not have to be recognized by the government, quality varies. Eighty-seven percent of India's 700,000 primary and secondary schools are in rural areas; but low teaching standards, high teacher absenteeism, sparse funding, lack of public services such as electricity and water, traditional gender bias, family poverty, and child malnutrition contribute to the 50 percent rural student dropout rate.

For children who remain in school, there is enormous pressure to be top of the class. Competition is a stressful component of childhood in India. Formal education and the stress on being "first rank" begins at the age of three. In nursery and kindergarten, children learn to read and write in their mother tongue and in Hindi or English. By the end of secondary school, at age seventeen or eighteen, students' vocational and educational options have been determined by their exam results. The cream of the crop may choose to attend one of India's top higher education institutions, such as an IIT (Indian Institute of Technology), or to become an International Student in the USA, the UK, Australia, Germany, or Canada.

If aptitude or exam results are not enough to qualify one's child for the desired Indian institution, "donations" or personal gifts can open the door. Corruption is a sad fact of educational life in India. Cheating on exams and papers are often viewed as a "right" rather than a wrong. Concerned families may pay tens of thousands of rupees to change the outcome of their son's or daughter's poor university entrance exam.

THE HOLY AND THE UNHOLY
There are groups of people living outside traditional family structures. Some are revered, others disdained, but all are kept at a distance and each one plays a valuable role in the very society that requires them to remain outside.

Sadhus
In a quest for personal enlightenment, millions of Indian men and women live as Hindu ascetics, or *sadhus*. Casting off family and communal responsibilities as well as worldly possessions and comforts, these voluntary outcastes can be seen in every corner of India. Considered "holy" by Hindus, *sadhus* are part of the Indian landscape.

Many *sadhus* are known for their spiritual teaching and are sought for blessing. A few evoke dread due to their occult powers and grotesque practices. Some wander alone, having taken a vow of silence. Others become part of a community devoted to a particular god, their divine allegiances identified by the color and pattern of forehead markings. It's common to see saffron-robed men sit along the street, wooden bowl in hand, begging for food or coins. During a festival you may see *Nagababas* ("naked fathers") parading en masse, with ash-covered bodies and long, matted hair. Revered by some as gods, feared because of their power to bless and to curse, *sadhus* are a visible reminder to Hindus of the unreality of the material world.

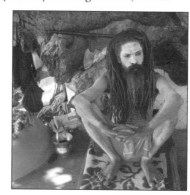

Hijras

Only in India is it possible to be simultaneously holy and unholy. *Hijras* embody this unique Indian perspective. Fifty thousand eunuchs (by birth, by force, or by choice) form transsexual, transvestite communities found mainly in the north. Living as a separate group, they are viewed as neither male nor female. They may "marry" within their community and form "families" of "sisters." They are not homosexual, though some work as male prostitutes. They follow a hierarchy that includes gurus, and can be punished and cast out for not following their own rules.

Using coarse language to embarrass, or making sexual advances to intimidate, *Hijras* solicit money from the public. Some show up uninvited, but not unexpectedly, at weddings. Payment leads to blessing newlyweds with fertility. Refusal results in verbal abuse and curses. When they sing and dance outside the home of a newborn boy, parents must pay them to avoid their child being cursed.

chapter six

TIME OUT

In India "leisure" depends very much on where one lives, one's status, family expectations, work demands, discretionary income, and accessibility to ideas and options. For village India and those whose lives are tied to the land, "leisure" is built into daily life and varies with the seasons. It varies even among the 25 percent of the population who live and work in towns and cities. Many work a six-day week. Some reserve a specific weekday for religious observances. For most, Saturday and Sunday are "the weekend."

On weekends, movie theaters are packed with groups of teenage friends and families. Indian families take short excursions by car or bus to nearby cities, visiting family or watching festival activities. They may visit a temple, take in a movie, and have a meal in a restaurant. For women who are responsible for a home and family, especially if they have a job outside the home, their "leisure" time may be consumed with meal preparation for family outings, housework, and other activities related to entertaining expected and unexpected visitors. Clubbing is common for the young middle classes in large metropolitan cities like Delhi, Mumbai, and Chennai.

Apart from the three official national holidays, employees may get fifteen to twenty vacation days a year; but recent shifts in the economy have pushed some companies to curtail holidays and increase work hours. Those who are fortunate enough to hold government jobs are less affected.

Many families get away for extended holidays during the hot summer months. In the past few years, vacationing abroad has become possible for India's middle class, or the affordable railways take people to popular destinations inside the country. Forested "hill stations," such as Mussoorie, Nainital, and Shimla in the north, or Ooty and Kodaikanal in the south, are fashionable with newlyweds.

EATING OUT

Everywhere you turn you'll find restaurants and *dhabbahs* (rustic outdoor cafés) serving regional, national, and international foods. American fast-food outlets, such as KFC and McDonalds, have become popular in the cities, offering country-specific menu items you won't find in the USA or Europe. For example, burgers in India are lamb, not beef, and there are always vegetarian options.

Restaurants have varying degrees of hygiene in the dining rooms and the kitchens. The cleanliness of the public eating area is probably a good indication of the standard in the kitchen. Visitors may need to make some adjustments. Since privacy and personal space are not of primary importance, be prepared to share a table.

TIPPING

Tipping is an acknowledgement of a job well done. In India, it is common practice in restaurants and hotels. In upscale eating establishments you may be charged a 15 to 20 percent "luxury tax" which is, essentially, a mandatory tip, and there's no need to add more. In other restaurants, just leave a few rupees rather than a percentage.

- Hotel porters may be tipped 5-10 rupees per bag, or when providing exceptional service.
- In most cases, taxi drivers and *dhabbah* waiters do not require a tip.
- Household servants, drivers, and those who regularly serve you can be given gifts of money on special occasions. In those situations it's understood as *baksheesh*—a gift made in advance in order to get the job done.
- If you are with Indian friends or colleagues, it's best to ask them about the normal practice in each instance and follow their lead.

Street Vendors

Ten million street vendors all over India sell food, and you need never go hungry if you have a few rupees. In south India, huge *dosai* (rice pancakes) fried in ghee (clarified butter) until crisp and filled with savory potatoes are sold on station platforms. Fruits and vegetables are deftly cut and beautifully presented, often wrapped in a banana leaf. Sugar cane juice is squeezed from huge roadside grinders straight into dubious-looking glasses. In north India boiled eggs sprinkled with salt, pepper, and chopped cilantro are sold during chilly winter evenings. *Chai* (tea) may be served in small clay cups that are dashed on the ground when finished. *Gol gupas, samosas, jalebis,* and a vast array of other tasty snacks and sweets ensure that you can eat your way through the streets of India.

Regional Dishes

Geography and religion shape India's cuisine. Rice is the staple in the south and northeast, where rainfall is the heaviest. Delicious flat breads are the mainstay in the central plains and the north, where wheat is grown. Coastal peoples eat fish. Food preparation and ingredients in the northeast are heavily influenced by their neighbor, China, and often include pork. In Muslim-influenced areas, you can dig into Mughlai-style food characterized by thick, rich curries sprinkled with nuts and dried fruit. Gujarati cuisine is typically sweeter than other regions, since many Gujarati cooks add jaggery (brown sugar) to balance the salt. *Thali* is a common lunch in Tamil Nadu. For a ridiculously low price, a huge stainless steel plate is filled with rice and small bowls of *rasam* (pepper soup), *sambhar* (vegetable stew), *dhal* (lentils), yogurt, a sampling of several vegetable dishes, a *chapatti* or *puri*, and a dessert. Andhra Pradesh is renowned for its fiery curries and the common practice of eating raw chilies as a side dish with rice.

Most Indians use chilies in cooking as well as in making pickles. Pickles are a necessity in Indian meals. The taste and type of pickle typically used varies not only regionally, but according to each home. Foreigners often need to acquire a taste for these pungent and usually spicy condiments.

India's unique sweets are worth sampling. Milk sweets, *gulab jamun* and *rasgulla, ras malai,* and *jalebis* are the most common. Then there are regional or local specialties, such as *petha*—candied winter melon (Uttar Pradesh) and *payasam*—milk cooked with sugar, nuts, and noodles (Kerala). For special occasions, *ladoo* (sweet nut and chickpea balls) and sweets covered with edible silver leaf are served.

Chai or coffee may be served after dinner, though these are usually treated as something to offer before breakfast or in between meals. *Chai* is a delicious blend of milk, tea, and sugar brought to a boil. On special occasions and in some regions spices such as cinnamon, cloves, or ginger are added. Indians serve "milk coffee" made with "Nescafe" (instant coffee), milk, and plenty of sugar. You can find "filtered coffee" in south India. "Black coffee" means coffee with sugar, no milk. So if you'd like coffee without sugar, make that clear.

FOOD CATEGORIES
Hot and Cold
If you're in India for any length of time, you will hear foods described as "hot" and "cold." This is not to be mistaken for spicy and non-spicy or warm and chilled foods. It is about a belief, rooted in Ayurvedic medicine, about what these foods do to your body. Older generations may give stern warnings about what you should and should not eat in different seasons, illnesses, or stages of life, based on this concept of "hot" and "cold."

Hot foods should never be eaten if pregnant because they can bring on miscarriage. Eating papaya, especially the seeds, is believed to be a surefire way to abort. After delivery of a baby, hot foods are required for recovery. They may include fruits and vegetables such as banana, pineapple, jackfruit, coconut, eggplant, and potatoes. Meat, fish, eggs, nuts, and, predictably, red chilies are hot. Mangoes should be eaten in moderation, since they are "hot" enough to cause boils. Dairy products should be avoided by new mothers, since yogurt, buttermilk, and other "cold" dairy products will give your baby digestive problems. "Cold" foods cannot be eaten in winter without making you sick.

Other instructions you'll hear: do not drink water just before or during a meal, don't drink milk after eating something sour, don't eat ice cream or drink cold drinks when it's cold outside or when you have a cold. All of these dietary restrictions are less well-known among the younger generations, but they may unthinkingly practice them since it is how their mothers and grandmothers raised them.

Clean and Unclean

There are other common food-related protocols that are in fact good practices for staying healthy in the Indian context. Nearly all Indians have "clean" and "unclean" foods. The most common "unclean" foods are all forms of meat for Hindus, pork for Muslims, and even for most Christians, and for some, shellfish and other scavengers.

Not just what one eats, but how, is important. The left hand is used for personal hygiene. The right hand only is used for serving and touching food. Left-handed children have been strictly trained to become right-handed. Indians may be shocked or disgusted if left-handed foreigners use their left hand to eat Indian-style. Ask for a fork!

Alcohol

Drinking alcohol is still viewed in Indian society as a vice. The majority of Indians don't drink, and it's often difficult to find a restaurant that serves alcohol. Before Independence, Gandhi prompted local governments to outlaw liquor, and various levels of prohibition lasted until 1977. Gujarat (where Gandhi was born) is the only "dry" state. Nationally it is illegal to advertise alcohol; but Western influence, the rise of consumerism, and the changes in family structures and disposable income have encouraged an increase in drinking among young urban professionals and women—though only 5 percent of Indian women drink.

In spite of a relatively small number of drinkers, bars are not uncommon. Typically, they are rough establishments frequented by local men. More upscale bars and clubs are found only in major cities such as Mumbai, Kolkata, Delhi, Bangaluru, Pondicherry, and Goa, where even underaged teens are (illegally) allowed access. Goa is also the only state where you'll find casinos.

The drinking age varies by state, ranging from eighteen in Uttar Pradesh, Karnataka, and Goa to twenty-five in Delhi. Most cities have early club curfews and some (such as Bangaluru) even ban dancing. Five-star hotels may be exempt, but expect to pay a cover charge and high prices.

Home-made drinks are common in rural areas. *Toddy* is wine made from the sap of the coconut palm flower. Sugarcane mash called *thara* is a 90-proof moonshine that can be deadly, and every year hundreds are poisoned by copper formaldehyde formed during distilling.

SPORTS AND GAMES

India's traditional sports and games are rooted in history. During the Vedic Period, noblemen were competent in a variety of manly pursuits, including wrestling and hunting. Battle skills were turned into sport, becoming archery, discus throwing, weightlifting, and wrestling.

Wrestling in India is not so much a sport as a way of life. Men dedicate themselves to the disciplines and gurus are required to learn the arts of *Pehlwani* (north India) or *Kalaripayat* (south).

Martial art forms that were the precursors to judo and karate originated in India and spread to Asia through Buddhist monks. Though these are not as widely practiced in India as in other Asian countries, India continues to win regional and international martial arts competitions.

Parcheesi, chess, playing cards, and snakes and ladders (known in the US as chutes and ladders) are very old Indian board games still played today.

Yoga

Self-realization in Hinduism requires an understanding of the physical and its relationship to the metaphysical. Yoga, meaning "union with Brahman," is a Hindu practice that has become a popular means of physical exercise in the West. It combines controlled breathing, specific postures, and withdrawal of the senses as a means of controlling the body and elevating the soul.

Kite Fighting

Kites are not just a child's plaything in India. Introduced by Chinese travelers, kite making and fighting are skills that have been passed on from father to son for centuries. *Patangs*—diamond-shaped bamboo and tissue paper constructions, maneuvered by a single string —are the most common. Hundreds of these colorful tailless kites can be seen flying from rooftops during Raksha Bandhan (see p. 13) and Independence Day. The aim is to cut the string of other kites, and to be the last kite flying. Ahmedabad's Kite Festival every January draws kite fighters from around the world.

Cricket

Although officially the national sport is hockey, Indians have a passion for cricket, and the Board of Control in India is the richest cricket board in the world. If there's a match going on, you can be sure that much of the country will be gathered around a TV set or a radio somewhere, cheering on their team.

Out and About

India's terrain invites everything from snorkeling to skiing. But Indians are not nature buffs. Camping and hiking are not common pastimes, even though there are eighty-nine national parks and more than 430 wildlife sanctuaries in India. Some of the most beautiful can be found in the Western Ghats of Kerala. The Himalayas stretch across the northern border of India. But you don't have to climb Mount Everest. A visit to Darjeeling or a short hike up the hills around Nainital offers breathtaking views.

The majority of Indians cannot swim. But people still picnic and play along India's many rivers, beautiful falls, and thousands of miles of coastline. Except in Goa and some of the more popular tourist beaches, Indian adults keep their clothes on, even if they venture into the water. If you plan to swim, be prepared to cover up and to be the center of attention no matter how you dress.

CULTURAL ACTIVITIES
Religion and History

India is a paradise for those interested in religion or history. Some religious celebration occurs nearly every day, and there is no shortage of sacred sites and cities. Five thousand years of recorded history make for fascinating discoveries all over the country.

Delhi and Agra make a wonderful introduction to Moghul history, complete with famous forts and, of course, the Taj Mahal. Cities famous for their temples and spiritual history, such as Varanasi, Sarnath, Bodhgaya, Haridwar, Amritsar, and Madurai, are popular tourist destinations for Indians as well as for foreigners.

Many of the holy places outside the more famous tourist routes may have more restrictions and be less tolerant of tourists. Should you wish to enter any religious building, leave your shoes outside and, if you're a woman, cover your head. If you are wearing shorts or a sleeveless shirt (whether male or female), put off your visit for another day when you are more appropriately dressed. Some temples and mosques will not permit those outside their religion to enter, so if you are not a Hindu or Muslim, check before you step inside.

If you keep your eyes open, you can spot India's smaller religious sites—its shrines. You may see them while crossing a bridge in south India, tucked under the base of a tree in north India, or on the crest of a hill in the mountain regions. Marked by a large, smooth stone or a carved statue, covered with garlands or snippets of marigolds, finger-painted with red powder or flanked with tiny oil candles, these sacred spots are home to gods, goddesses, saints, or spirits who are treated as local deities and worshiped and appeased. People come offering sweets and flowers, seeking protection or blessing. These shrines are often adjacent to temples of better-known deities.

The Arts
Art is intrinsic to Indian life. The richness and beauty of its cultural diversity are manifest in its ancient architecture, paintings, music, dance, and handicraft skills, as well as in the plethora of contemporary art, music, fashion, and cinema.

Music
For millennia the intensity, passion, devotion, and poetry of the Indian peoples have been poured into the world through music. Both musician and listener can become caught up in the experience, as all the senses are engaged by intricate sound patterns, rich color, exotic dance,

clapping crowds, and pungent incense. For most people outside India, the subtleties and beauty of India's classical music may require an adjustment of both mind and heart. But that, as we will see, is the purpose of this music.

The tonal foundation for the composition of all of Indian classical and much of contemporary music is the *raag* (Hindi) or *ragam* (Tamil), meaning "color" or "passion." A *raag* is a five-to-seven-note series used to form a melody. Unlike Western music, Indian classical music has no absolute pitch. The musician chooses a note from which all other notes follow. *Tal*—the rhythm—is the second necessary element. A third element—the "drone"—is usually played on a stringed instrument called a *tanpura*. The drone grounds the music, creating harmonics by plucking resonating notes that run like a thread through an entire song or piece.

Raag and *Tal* form the foundation of the two strains of Indian classical music. The intricacy of classical *sangeet* (music or songs) takes a lifetime to learn and requires the guidance of a guru. Hindustani Sangeet, in the north, is distinctly influenced by Persia and Islam. The most famous Indian instruments, the *sitar* and the *tabla*, are Hindustani. But many other stringed and percussion instruments are common. Carnatic Sangeet, from south India, focuses on vocals accompanied by violin, *veena* (a type of lute), and other stringed and wind instruments.

Improvisation is a unique aspect of Indian classical music. It is an art to be mastered through instruction, discipline, and secrets imparted by one's guru. Nothing compares to the beauty, competition, and sheer joy of watching a battle of the *sitars* or listening to vocalists challenge one another to imitate spontaneous compositions of mind-boggling complexity.

Much of India's music has been written to express religious devotion. *Bhajans* are simple, poetic songs or chants usually heard in or near temples and at religious events. *Kirtans* are *bhajans* sung antiphonally as leader calls to listeners, who sing their reply.

Ghazals, imported to India from Persia, can be spiritual songs, but are more often romantic recitations set to music. Ghalib, India's most famous *ghazal* writer, began composing when he was ten years old, and eventually became court poet for the last Mughal Emperor of Delhi.

Film songs (*filmi sangeet*) make up 72 percent of India's music sales. Many of them have never even been in a movie, but they have become so popular that this is now a separate genre label for the style.

Indian pop music (Indipop) arose in the late 1970s and continues to evolve. It spices up Indian classical and folk styles, remixes film classics, and has added hip-hop to its ingredients to create a flavor all its own.

Dance
Vocals and instruments are often accompanied by dance. Eight regional dance forms are accepted in India as "classical." *Kathak*, meaning "storyteller," developed in North India during the Mughal period and was originally performed by courtesans in the courts of kings. *Kathakali* (Kerala) tells the stories of the Hindu epics, *Ramayana* and *Mahabharata*, and the ancient *Puranas. Manipuri* (Manipur) depicts tales of the life of Lord Vishnu. *Sittriya* (Assam) is a fifteenth-century dance form honoring Vishnu. *Mohiniaattam* (Kerala) is the dance of Vishnu's enchanting female avatar, Mohini. *Sattriya Kuchipudi* (Andhra Pradesh), uniquely characterized by

movement combined with speech, dramatizes Hindu mythology. *Odissi* is the oldest Indian classical dance. Carvings of Odissi dancers can be found on the Sun Temple at Konark. *Odissi* (Orissa) and *Bharatanatyam* (Tamil Nadu) are the only two classical forms considered "temple dances." They were historically performed by *devadasis*—young girls who served priests and entertained the elite, having been given by their families in "marriage" to a god.

There are myriad forms of folk dance, many of which are still performed during religious and seasonal festivals as well as for special community occasions. Colorful costumes and traditional headdresses or jewelry add swirl and sparkle to these local and tribal dances.

Movies

Cinema is one of India's most renowned art forms. A thousand films are cranked out annually, and not all of them from Bollywood. With volume that high, it's no wonder that a majority are based on standard formulae— boy loves girl from afar, boy meets girl, tragedy strikes, and either love overcomes all or no one lives happily ever after. Of course there is always song and dance, sometimes when you least expect it. But that can be what makes Hindi movies entertaining, even if you don't understand the language.

Worthy films should not get lost in the crowd. Hindi, Tamil, Bengali, Kannada, Malayalam, Marathi, and Telugu cinema continue to produce acclaimed works of art. *The Apu Trilogy*, three Bengali films directed by Satyajit Ray in the late 1950s, won numerous awards, and these are recognized to be among the best movies of all time.

Not all films are based on original scripts. Many are not-so-cloaked remakes of classic movies or stories from the West. *Black* (2005) is partially based on Helen Keller's story. *Bride and Prejudice* (2004) is an entertaining version of the Jane Austen novel. Movies like these have made Indian cinema accessible for much of the rest of the world. The music and fashion of Indian cinema are also influencing Western popular culture.

In India, both theaters and theatergoers have changed over the past few years, and Indian movies are changing in response. Multiscreen cinemas have replaced movie houses. More than 350 million Indians speak English, in addition to one or more Indian languages. Satellite TV and the Internet have opened the door to other kinds of big- and small-screen productions. An increase in income and leisure time among the middle class has been a boon to the movie industry. What was previously a place for young males to congregate once a month has now become respectable for a weekly family outing.

At the end of the twentieth century, big-budget productions took a dive. Finding it less feasible to finance the requisite song and dance routines, the film industry looked for a solution. They found it in English and export.

The first English language film in India was made in 1931 with the advent of "talkies." In the 1980s and '90s many English films were made; but the themes were still standard *masala* (typical Bollywood fare). Today increasing numbers of movies are being made in English and Hinglish—a linguistic and cultural mix of Hindi and English. These films, often produced or directed by NRI's (nonresident Indians), express the personal identity, generational conflicts, social struggles, and range of emotions of Indians swept up in massive culture shift. Movies

like *Hyderabad Blues* (1998), *Monsoon Wedding* (2001), *Mitr, My Friend* (2002), and *Via Darjeeling* (2008) convey the new realities of the generation now stepping into adulthood.

Should you take in a movie while in India, prepare yourself to enjoy a community experience. Talking throughout, cell phones ringing, cheering on the hero, or singing along would not be considered rude or unusual. So go with the flow and have fun. It is all part of the India experience.

For the most part Indian movies do not contain potentially offensive material. The Central Board of Film Certification makes sure that scenes involving sex, violence, and political subversion end up on the cutting-room floor. A few movies in the past decade have been banned altogether.

India's movie rating system has three categories: U (Unrestricted Public Exhibition) for family viewing, U/A (unrestricted Public Exhibition with parental guidance for children under twelve) for mild violence, language, and sensuality, and A (Adult) for those over eighteen only. There is also a rare S rating for "specialized audience," such as for doctors only. If a film says "no rating" it has been banned from public exhibition.

Indian shops, inside and outside the country, carry plenty of DVDs, many of them pirated. Eighty million pirated DVDs are sold every year. You can usually spot them by the grainy printing of the covers. If you fail to notice it in the shop, you will discover it in the poor sound and picture quality when you view it at home. US $400 to 500 million are lost to the movie and music industries every year through film piracy in India. Antipiracy laws do exist. Those who breach them in India can face up to three years in prison and a fine of up to 200,000 rupees—fourteen times the per capita income. But in reality most offenders get away with paying only a small fine, and go back to making more illegal copies.

Literature

The Hindu epics and other Sanskrit scriptures, originally sung or recited in order to transmit them from one generation to the next, are fascinating literary works, regardless of your religious beliefs. Ancient poetry, such as the twelfth-century *Gitagovinda* ("The Cowherd's Song") and the works of the fourteenth-century poets Tulasidas and Kabir Das, are still known and recited.

Though many think of Sanskrit as the primary literary language, classical literature has been written in all of India's languages. Tamil predates Sanskrit, beginning in the first century CE. A. K. Ramanujan is famous for translating Tamil classics into English. Gandhi wrote his autobiography, *My Experiments with Truth*, 1929, in Gujarati. Bengali was the language of Rabindranath Tagore, who was awarded the Nobel Prize for Literature in 1913.

In the post-British era, English has been a recognized medium of classic Indian literature, too. R. K. Narayan writes of south Indian village life. Mulk Raj Anand's novels are social protest. Salman Rushdie became infamous overnight with the publication of *The Satanic Verses*. Arundhati Roy won the Booker Prize for *The God of Small Things*. Anita Desai, whose latest novel is *The Zig Zag Way*, is known for her powerful and in-depth portrayal of her central female characters.

Rabindranath Tagore composed more than 2,200 songs, including India's national anthem. His unique adaptation of Indian classical and folk music led to the emergence of a new genre: Rabindra Sangeet. His music, poetry, and perspective shaped not only Indian music, but also its history and culture.

SHOPPING FOR PLEASURE

Most Indians shop out of necessity rather than for pleasure. Though city malls exist, most people shop in the traditional way. Goods of a similar nature are sold by rows of shopkeepers in the same vicinity. You go to the spice market for spices, the fish market for fish, the gold *gully* (lane) for gold, and the plastic lane or stainless steel area for boxes, utensils, shelving, and waste bins.

If shopping is your interest, you will find more than enough to occupy your time. Each region has its own specialty. Rajasthan offers mirror-work hangings, papier-

mâché puppets, traditional shoes with curled toes, jewelry, and antique furniture. Sandalwood soaps, incense, and carvings are famous in Karnataka. Varanasi and Chennai are both known for silk, and Kashmir for embroidered shawls and clothing. Unique fabrics, classical instruments, Darjeeling teas, and spices are other items you might want to take home. You can buy them locally or find everything in Delhi's excellent emporiums.

Shopping hours and closed days are variable. Some shops close on Mondays, others on Fridays or Sundays. It depends on the religious beliefs of the shop owner, holidays celebrated, and family needs and circumstances.

The Shopping Experience

A woman's first priority in India may be to find a tailor who can "stitch" the latest in *shalwar-kameez* fashion. Cotton, "terry-cot" (cotton-polyester blend), or silk outfits can be made to suit style, figure, and purse. Ready-made clothes are also available.

While shopping you may encounter the Indian unwillingness to say "no." To say "no" to you is to lose his reputation as well as a relationship with you as a customer. Some shopkeepers will try all manner of dodges, expecting you to understand that they do not have what you're asking for. It's your responsibility as the customer to get the message. They may try to sell you something else. You might be told to "come back tomorrow." (If you do, it will still not be there.) Or, if you're lucky, he'll say, "Wait one minute." In a few minutes, he'll reappear with what you want, having run down the street to find it at another store.

Shopping for personal mementos or for gifts for people back home, you have two possibilities: buying in a government handicraft shop or "emporium," where prices are fixed, or bargaining practically everywhere else.

What Not To Do

I'd never seen anyone go into the shop around the corner from my house, but I couldn't go on ignoring the shimmering gold *zari* (threads) woven boldly into the bright red cotton, and the translucent orange silk with the gold fringe hanging at the shop door.

Why did the man look at me so oddly as I admired the designs? Shopkeeper aren't usually so standoffish. Then someone tapped me on the shoulder. I turned around to see a woman, who smiled and told me in English, "This shop sells cloth to cover dead bodies. I don't think you mean to shop here." Shocked and embarrassed, I thanked her and moved away.

That day I learned two important things: when in a cross-cultural situation, observe, ask questions, and copy not only what people do, but what they don't do; and it's a rare and kind person who will discreetly point out a cultural faux pas to a foreigner!

Bargaining

Most shopkeepers expect you to bargain, but you should only begin the process if you truly intend to buy. You can get a feel for prices by visiting other stores first, including government stores, where the prices are fixed. However, you will still be charged more than the locals, so try to take an Indian friend with you and let him or her do the talking. You'll save some money and get a bit of training to improve your own bargaining skills for the next time.

Look at several things, and ask the shopkeeper about them. When you find what you want, don't seem too interested. Ask the cost, and say, "Is that your best price?" He will suggest slightly less. You can then say, "Oh, that's too much!" He may ask, "What will you pay?" State a figure that is half or even a third of the original price, intending to pay a little more. If he refuses, move toward the door. He will probably come down a little, you go up a little, and carry on until you reach a price acceptable to you both. Don't leave unless you're willing to lose your find. If you return, he'll ask the full price. In some places you can pay less than half the asking price, especially if you're buying in quantity, or if you're the first customer of the day (considered auspicious). But abusing this by suggesting a ridiculous price will only generate ill will. So keep it light and fun, and remember that they're trying to make a living.

Reality Check

Synthetic fabrics are often called "silk" in India. Before buying you should know the test for real silk. Ask the shopkeeper to pull out a thread from the edge of the fabric. Light it with a match. If the ash is black and smells like burning hair, it's silk. If it is chalky and smells like burning paper, it's rayon. Polyester melts into little beads. If he is reluctant to oblige, you can draw your own conclusions.

Exchanging Money

Because of the hassle and expense of exchanging money, it may be in your best interest to change a large amount in the airport at the start of your journey. US dollars and British pounds are the easiest to exchange. You can use credit cards and traveler's checks in major cities; ATMs and foreign-exchange kiosks can be found in many places; but using rupees is trouble free. Traveler's checks are not accepted everywhere. If there is a power outage or your credit cards are lost or stolen, you will need cash.

A word of warning: there are many unauthorized money changers. For your protection, don't exchange money with anyone who approaches you on the street. Use airport exchange services or a bank. Banking hours are 10:00 a.m. to 2:00 p.m., Monday through Friday. Expect to wait in line, and have your passport ready.

SAFE SIGHTSEEING

Buses, trains, and tour companies carry millions of people to India's famous historical, religious, and vacation spots. Interspersed with Indian tourists and pilgrims are foreign tourists and vacationing expats, conspicuous whether on a group tour bus or navigating trains and taxis on their own. You are likely to encounter unauthorized tour guides, beggars, pickpockets, and con artists.

Tour guides offer their services to individuals or small groups. Authorized guides should have identification, but badges can be faked. Often brochures provided at a historical site will give information about tours and tour guides, including fees. Don't give money in advance; don't allow anyone to hold your belongings, drag you into a souvenir shop, coerce you into taking a taxi to another site, or talk you into paying more at the end of the tour than was originally quoted. Those may all be indicators that you are being set up for theft, or worse. Dirty, smiling children may chat in English in a friendly attempt to extract a few rupees from you. If you are jostled on the street, your pocket has probably been picked, as Indians can and do avoid physical contact with others except in the most crowded situations.

A FEW TOP SPOTS

There are so many cultural and natural attractions in India that it's impossible to do it all justice, but there are a few spots that should not be missed.

North

Old and New Delhi are a "must." **Agra** is filled with

architectural wonders, from the Taj Mahal and the Agra Fort to nearby Fatehpur Sikri.

Kashi (now Varanasi) is one of the world's oldest living cities. Millions of pilgrims travel each month to this most holy Hindu place on the Ganges. Nearby **Sarnath** is the site of the Ashoka Pillar, marking the spot where Buddha preached his first sermon.

Nainital is one of the many beautiful hill stations. Hike to see the Himalayas, go boating on the peaceful Naini Lake, or visit Sri Aurobindo Ashram (religious community). Visit the Jim Corbett National Park, nearby.

Khajuraho has Hindu temples and erotic sculptures.

East and Northeast

In **Kolkata**, you can visit Mother Teresa's Home for the Destitute and Dying. At the adjacent Kalighat Temple, animal sacrifices are offered to the goddess Kali.

On the Darjeeling Himalayan Railway, the "Toy Train" runs by steam from **Siliguri** to **Darjeeling**, with views of the Himalayas.

In **Assam**, visit the Kaziranga National Park, which has the largest number of Indian rhinos and hosts the Elephant Festival.

South

Kochi (Cochin) has Chinese fishing nets and the Kerala backwaters, along with the only Jewish settlement still in existence in India.

Madurai has the Sri Meenakshi and Sundareswarar Temples, epitomizing South Indian Hindu architecture.

Cape Comorin, or **Kanniyakumari**, is the southernmost tip of the Indian peninsula, where the Bay of Bengal, the Arabian Sea, and the Indian Ocean meet.

West

At **Jaipur**, the beautiful "Pink City," you can find the Tiger Fort (Nahargah Fort).

Goa has the best-known beaches, but don't miss the numerous wildlife sanctuaries and the Dudhsagar ("Milk Sea") Falls.

TRAVEL, HEALTH, & SAFETY

In terms of transportation, India's got it all: planes, trains, buses, taxis, cars, scooters, camels, elephants, bullock carts, horse-drawn *tongas*, along with auto, cycle, and human rickshaws. The rapid growth of the economy since the early 1990s has been matched by ever-growing demands on transportation infrastructure and services. Though travel within the country is relatively inexpensive, poor roads, an aging railway system, chaotic airports, and a general lack of order and sanitation make it a challenge. The government is working to improve national highways, rural roads, and road maintenance. The World Bank is also investing heavily in road and rail upgrades, and airports are privatizing in order to make headway on the ground and in the air.

Navigating India's transportation options as well as looking after yourself and your property during your travels will require effort. But equipped with the right

information, a good attitude, and a willingness to ask for help, traveling itself will be an unforgettable and even treasured part of your stay in India.

VISAS

All visitors, except for those from Nepal and Bhutan, require a visa that, in most cases, must be obtained prior to entering the country. Tourist visas are good for up to six months. There is a five-year tourist visa, but these long-term "tourists" can only stay for three months at a time.

Tourists can no longer lengthen their stay by making "visa runs" to neighboring countries. Even long-term, multi-entry tourist visa holders must remain outside the country for two months before returning. These laws are not consistently applied, and there are exceptions. Visitors should contact the Indian Consulate General in their own country before arrival, or check with their Embassy in India if they plan to leave and reenter the country.

ARRIVAL

Brace yourself for impact when arriving in India. The sensory overload of crowd, sound, and smell can cause even experienced travelers to question their skills and their sanity. Airports are chaotic.

Stepping outside, the heat hits you like a wave. You will be engulfed in a swarm of taxi-walas vying for your business. Scruffy-looking children tug on your sleeve, looking for a handout. The smell of pollution tinged with urine is overwhelming, the decibel level is deafening, and the full assault on body and mind can be exhausting, making it hard to think. For this reason, some decisions about what to do next should be made ahead of time: advance preparation will alleviate some of the stress you'll encounter on arrival in India.

AIR TRAVEL

India has twelve international airports, and many local ones. The government-owned Indian Airlines had a monopoly until 2005, when private companies were allowed to operate. Competition has fueled better fares and services.

Flying within the country is still a high-priced option, especially for short distances. But that has not deterred Indian or foreign travelers. With the rise in private airlines, air travel volume has tripled. This is good for those wishing to go more places faster, but not so good for India's airports, which lack the infrastructure to handle the rapid growth on runways and in terminals. This is especially true for Delhi and Mumbai, which handle 50 percent of India's air traffic.

BY ROAD

Roads still carry 90 percent of the travelers and 65 percent of the freight in India. While the number of roads has increased over the past fifty years, road quality has not.

India has around 1,865,000 miles (around 3 million km) of roads. But they are poorly made and maintained, narrow, and congested, especially those in metropolitan areas. According to the World Bank only 20 percent of India's roads are in decent condition. During monsoon season, flooded roads cut off 40 percent of the population, primarily in villages in the north and northeast, from the rest of the country.

Taxis

Prepaid taxis are the safest way to go from the airport or railway station to your hotel or guesthouse. You will be assured of a legitimate driver and the standard fare—

visible on the meter. While tipping is not necessary, a small fee per item of luggage may be added on to the fare. Ask at the prepaid counter.

Newer cars are invading taxi territory. But most cabs are still the yellow or yellow and black Premier Padminis and Hindustan Ambassadors, both made since the mid-1950s and not air-conditioned. The company making Premier Padminis went out of business in the late 1990s. But these old cars are still the reliable rulers of India's roads. Slogans painted along the top of each taxi—"*Allah hu Akbar*," "*Ram Satya Nam*," or "Jesus is Lord"— advertise the driver's religious affiliation. Inside the taxi you'll see his family photos pinned to the visor, small pictures of his gods or religious symbols on the window or glued to the dashboard, and religious paraphernalia meant to ward off the evil eye hanging from the rearview mirror. While you're looking around, note the driver's name and ID number on his posted license, in the unlikely event that you encounter a problem.

En route, the driver may tell you that he can't find your hotel or that it's fully booked, and will offer to take you to a different hotel. It's a scam. If he insists he doesn't know the place, tell him to take you back to the prepaid counter to get another taxi. Do not give him the receipt you received from the prepaid counter until he sets you down at your desired destination or takes you back to where you came from. That receipt ensures he gets paid. Make sure he's earned it.

Most cab drivers speak enough English to understand your destination and tell you how much you owe, though the meter will show you the fare, too. Some drivers might offer to give you a tour of the city en route to your destination. If they've been especially helpful or appropriately friendly, feel free to give them a tip. If you're not interested in being chatty, pretend to sleep or simply stop paying attention.

Taxis can be hired on a regular basis to drive you to work or school, or while you're visiting a city as a tourist. In general they can be relied on to show up at the right time and get you where you want to go without difficulty. A taxi driver may ask if he can pick up other passengers on the way. While this is a common practice, for your safety and peace of mind it's perfectly all right to decline.

Auto Rickshaws

Cheaper and more maneuverable than taxis, India's yellow and black auto rickshaws are ubiquitous. Doorless three-wheel cabs on a motorcycle engine, these tiny vehicles have been known to carry a dozen people—but you don't have to share.

These open autos are no protection from pollution in congested traffic. Carry a handkerchief or light scarf to wrap around your nose and mouth and enjoy the up close and personal views afforded by this fun mode of transportation. For those with asthma or other health concerns, they may not be the best choice.

RULES OF THE ROAD

My parents came to India for a two-month visit. After a couple of weeks my father understood India's rules of the road: "There are only two. 1. Fill every possible space; and 2. The biggest vehicle has the right of way."

Driving

India's auto industry is growing fast, the number of cars on the road increasing by 15 percent per year. Tata, Hindustan Motors, and Maruti, India's main manufacturers, have been joined by Ford, Honda, Fiat, and other foreign companies looking for a share of the market.

Driving is best left to the Indians, but you can rent a car, with or without a driver, in any major city. There are official rules and regulations posted by the Department of Road Transport and Highways, and you should be aware of these. Driving is on the left side of the road.

Roads are narrow and riddled with potholes. Cows and dogs take up a good share of the road, even in cities. Center lines or lane markers do not mean much, and any gap is a possible "lane." Turn signals are rare. Horns blare. Policemen may direct traffic at a junction even with a working stoplight, simply because lights may be ignored. Expect to find yourself in a knot of traffic at some time during your travels that will require the untangling expertise of a few fearless men.

Should you be in an accident or stopped for some reason by police, severe fines and/or imprisonment could be in store—though a reasonable bribe will probably not be declined.

Although public transportation systems are at least adequate throughout India, you may want to hire a car with a driver if you'd like to go at your own pace or get to a remote spot without the inevitable crowds and delays of bus travel or the geographic restrictions of a taxi. Hiring a car and driver is relatively inexpensive and will still provide enough thrills to suit any adrenalin junkie.

Buses

Buses are a cheap way to get around the country, but you get what you pay for: constant stops, cramped seats, bumpy roads, and no "facilities" either on the bus or at bus stations.

City buses are overcrowded, chaotic, and dirty. Everyone pushes and shoves to get inside, and it's often impossible to maneuver enough elbow room to take change from your pocket or purse to pay the fare. Sometimes the conductor can't even get through. When that happens you pass your fare to the conductor via other passengers.

Pickpockets invisibly conduct their business in the press of the crowd. You may get off at your stop to realize you are missing your wallet, jewelry, or handbag. Women standing in the aisles may be groped and must figure out how to defend themselves against both pickpockets and perverts.

City buses may not always come to a complete halt. If you hesitate to jump off at your stop, the oncoming crowds may push you back inside the bus, where you'll be stuck until you work up the nerve to press through again to the door and fling yourself off at the next stop.

Long-distance buses often show nonstop films and videos, not all of them suitable for children. At bus stations, vendors of all ages jump on to sell cold drinks, *chai*, and snacks. Beggars rush to the windows asking for money or food. If you need to get off the bus, check with the driver first. Ask him to wait for you to return, or you may find yourself stranded without your luggage. Don't expect to find a toilet anywhere en route!

A few Rapid Transit systems are working to improve buses and their services, including the addition of new buses and air-conditioning. But for the most part, buses are dirty, cramped, and late.

Pedestrians

The most difficult thing you may be required to do while in India is cross the road. Pedestrians do not have the right of way. When there is a space in the traffic, head for the middle of road and wait again while cars, scooters, autos, and buses speed past. Your safest course of action is to wriggle your way into the middle of a crowd and go with the flow.

Accidents

Road accidents are the major cause of accidental death in India. Currently thirteen people die every hour, 1.3 million are injured on the streets every year, and these numbers rise annually. Speeding, drunk driving, and disregard for seat belts or helmets are the main factors.

Aggression is part of the driving experience. Fourteen percent of India's drivers report being assaulted in road-rage incidents. Irritation, shouting, and gesturing mount, especially during the hot season. Do not respond in kind. Though it rarely happens to foreigners, mobs have been known to exact a justice of their own. So don't get out of your car if confronted by an angry driver, even if there has been an injury (whether you caused it or not). Solicit the help of people from the crowd that will inevitably gather to calm the aggressor and to give you advice.

BY RAIL

Asia's largest rail system, the government-owned Indian Railways, has nearly 40,000 miles (64,000 kilometers) of track woven through the whole of India. Around 7,000 trains carry 11 to 14 million passengers per day. Delhi and Kolkata have underground Metros. Other major cities carry on with the commuter trains put on the tracks by the British. Safer and cheaper than flying, traveling by train is a fascinating way to experience India.

Class Options

There are several classes of rail travel, though not all are available on every train.

Second Class (Unreserved)

For a close encounter with "the real India" this is the place to be. No reservation is required to travel second class. Coaches are divided into multiple compartments, each designed to seat six people, but traveling without a reservation means that as many people as possible squeeze in. As a foreigner traveling in Second Class, you will be an attraction, adding to the number of people who desire to sit as close to you as possible. Compartments have an aisle, beyond which is another seat meant for two. Don't choose a seat on the aisle, as constant traffic means that your feet and luggage are in the way and your belongings are an easy target for thieves.

Third Class (Unreserved)
People fill every possible space, with more entering the train at every station, requiring you to move over, take up even less room, and be even more alert about watching your belongings. The uncomfortable wooden seats and the cramped conditions make long-distance travel in this class something you may want to avoid.

Sleeper Class
While still crowded, noisy, and not so clean, Sleeper Class requires reservations, assuring travelers of a padded seat during the day and a berth at night. Each coach has multiple compartments, each with six berths and two additional berths along the aisle, making for close traveling companions. If you have the misfortune to book an aisle

berth, you'll discover at night when you put your "bed" down that it is enclosed at both ends, making it considerably shorter than the ones in the six-person section. In the compartment, center berths are folded up against the wall during the day to allow relatively comfortable seating. Unless you've reserved the upper berth that remains down twenty-four hours a day, don't expect to stretch your legs or be able to take a midday nap.

Air-Conditioned: 3A, 2A, 1A

Three Tiered Air-Conditioned Class (3A) has sealed, tinted windows, extra padded berths, and, of course, air-conditioning. Compartments here are also open, but the train car itself is locked at night and protected by the conductor, who makes sure that no unauthorized vendors or passengers enter. A sheet, a thin woolen blanket, and a pillow are provided, as are meals, if you have reserved them at the time you purchased your ticket.

Two Tiered Air-Conditioned Class (2A) is the same as 3A, but with only four berths per compartment and two along the aisle. Curtains can be pulled across your berth, giving privacy at night as you sleep.

First-Class Air-Conditioned Class (1A) tickets costs as much as an air fare. Unlike all the other options, each two-

or four-berth compartment is closed with a door that can be locked from the inside. There are no aisle berths.

Some day trains have AC Chair Cars, which is like economy air travel. Because they are air-conditioned and relatively cheap, they're a better option for many than second class. Toilets tend to be cleaner in all of the AC classes. The only downside to traveling AC occurs if the train breaks down en route. Then you're stuck in a closed car with windows that cannot be opened.

In most of these classes, don't be surprised to have to wrestle your way on to the train only to find someone else in your assigned seat. People usually wait for the boarding chaos to die down before adjusting themselves into the right spaces. If you have a problem with someone who refuses to leave your seat or who says they have the same seat, simply wait for the conductor to come and resolve it. (Don't leave your luggage to go and look for him, unless you have locked your bags to the underside of the seat. Make sure you take your hand luggage, passport, and cash with you.)

DO'S AND DON'TS OF HARASSMENT

If you are harassed on a train:
- Don't expect a polite verbal rebuke to solve the problem.
- Do enlist help from a man traveling with a wife or family.
- Don't assume you've done anything wrong.
- Do tell train officials immediately. Ask to register the incident in the official complaint book.
- Don't become paranoid.
- Do appreciate the vast majority of decent men, who will treat you with respect and come to your aid in a fatherly or brotherly fashion.

Ladies Only

Commuters jostle for space. For women it's often an unpleasant, if not humiliating, experience. In response to this need, many suburban trains have "Ladies' Compartments." These are often located at either end of a train, and may be hard to find and harder to enter, especially during morning rush hours. It's not uncommon for men to force their way into compartments marked "Ladies only" to find a seat or to harass, molest, or rob female passengers. There are also complaints made about *hijras* (eunuchs) feeling free to sit in the ladies' section.

Delhi, Mumbai, Kolkata, and Chennai have introduced women-only trains called "Ladies' Specials." Well-lit, brightly painted coaches have been designed for the comfort and security of working women and students, with five female constables and three male officers on patrol. If Ladies' Specials prove successful, more will be introduced elsewhere.

Reservations

Reservations can be made in advance for all classes of accommodation: via the Internet (expect technical problems), at a station (expect long lines), or through a travel agent (expect a small fee). Reservations are not required for second or third class. Ladies' queues are usually available. Look for the sign, or a line of women only.

Train timetables may be difficult to read, and station names are not city names. Prices for the same destination may vary, based on travel time or route. Passenger trains can be very slow, stopping at every station; express trains are twice as fast, but require reservations made weeks in advance. Don't be shy about asking for help to decipher timetables, posted information, or the system.

Tourist Counters and Quotas

At larger stations there will be a separate Tourist Office where only foreigners are allowed to book tickets in air-

conditioned comfort with people who can answer any
questions. You may need to pay in cash to buy a ticket in
the tourist office. Cash payments will require your
passport and US dollars, British pounds sterling, or rupees
if you can show a bank receipt for exchange transactions.
Trains are typically full, so whenever possible, book in
advance. But there is a tourist quota, making it
occasionally possible to find a berth even during peak
months or in an emergency. If there is no Tourist Office,
ask to speak with the person in charge of the station—
usually the Station Superintendent or the Station Master.
They have the power to sell you Tourist, VIP, or Emergency
Quota tickets when available.

RAC
RAC, or "Reservation Against Cancellation" means that
you've been placed on a waiting list for a sleeper berth.
(It is not the same as "Wait Listed," which simply means
you're waiting for an RAC.) Arrive at the station early to
find the passenger list on the reservation board. If your
name is on the list, you have a seat, though this does not
assure you of a berth. You can speak to the Station
Manager about Emergency or VIP quota options that may
be available an hour before departure.

Do not get on a train for an overnight journey without
a reservation. There will probably be no berth or seat
available. You can be put off the train or forced to stand or
sit outside the toilet at the end of the car. Not only is it
uncomfortable, it's unsafe, especially for women.

Luggage and Coolies
Luggage allowance on trains is similar to that on airlines.
How much you can take depends on your ticket class, so
be sure to ask about it when you purchase your ticket.
Overweight baggage will cost you dearly. Coolies (porters)
wearing red shirts and badges are available to carry your

luggage at every railway station. They will approach you with a smile and offer to carry your bags for an exorbitant price. If you want one to put your bags on the train (rather than just on the platform), establish this up front. After a bit of haggling, he may pick up your bags, telling you to pay whatever you wish, but don't hand them over until you have agreed upon a price. It's worth a few rupees to have the expert help. He will lock them under the seat for you if you have a chain and lock handy. Purchase these before your train journey.

Always lock your luggage under the seat on an overnight train trip. Before your destination, the conductor will alert you to prepare to disembark. Or ask other passengers to tell you when you're nearing the station. That is the time to unlock your luggage, gather your belongings and your ticket, and move toward the door. As you enter the station, coolies will spot you and run to help you get your luggage down and find a taxi.

It is possible to check in your bags at the start of your train trip. They will be put in a separate baggage compartment and unloaded at your destination for you to collect at the designated baggage office. It is, however, best to take them with you on the train, even though it seems like a hassle. The wait and the possible bribe required to collect them are rarely worth the "convenience" of checking them in, unless you have excess baggage that will not fit under your seat.

On the Train

Train journeys between north and south can take three or more days. It's three days well spent if you're interested in culture or language learning, enjoying the landscape, or simply want a very Indian experience.

At every station, unless you're in an AC or women's carriage that is locked or guarded, the aisles will fill up with Indian Railway approved *chai-walas* and snack vendors. It's a good idea to carry small bills and change for any items you wish to purchase. If you smell something delicious at a station and want to get off to buy a snack, check with someone to make sure the train stops long enough for you to disembark, make your purchase, and still make it back on the train.

Most people traveling by train bring their own food. Ticket holders for overnight journeys can buy meals onboard. Check at the station when you purchase your ticket or with the conductor once you're on the train. Basic vegetarian meals are served. Soon after departure, someone will take your order for dinner (served after 8:00 or 9:00 p.m.) and for breakfast the next morning. There are no dining cars. Meals are brought to you in your compartment. Don't expect to sit up late. After dinner, everyone will retire. If you don't get the hint, you will be asked politely to stand up while people lower their berths and adjust their bedding.

You may find yourself the only woman in an all-male compartment or occupying a berth across the aisle from a person of the opposite sex. In this country, where privacy is not an issue, no one thinks anything of it.

Expect to be awoken early by the *chai-wala* asking if you'd like hot milk coffee or *chai*. People will head for the bathrooms in the early morning to wash and brush their teeth before taking food.

Using the toilet on a train is an experience. Squatting over a hole with a view of the speeding tracks is motivation to use the handrail—even if you're squeamish about who touched it last. Even Western-style toilets may have been used as a squat toilet by villagers unaccustomed to that foreign utility. If the toilet in your car is not clean enough, try the next car. Squat toilets are cleaner. But if you've never used one, you'd better practice before taking a train trip. Extra dexterity and strength are required to balance on a moving train. Toilet use is not allowed at stations;

nevertheless, some stations have sweepers working full-time on the tracks to clear waste left by trains and their passengers.

Although Indian Railways is working to keep all but authorized passengers and vendors off their trains, others do manage to enter. Children or adults sweep up compartment floors, asking for "tips." Performers sing or dance in the aisles, hoping to be paid for entertaining. Pickpockets and thieves find a way in, too. Keep documents and cash concealed on your person at all times. If someone new appears to be eyeing you or your luggage, say something to the people with whom you're traveling and point out the person to the conductor. At night, keep your head, your jewelry, and any small bags away from open windows. Thieves standing on the platform have been known to reach through the window bars to pull earrings out of pierced ears.

In the midst of crowds and necessary cautions, don't miss the people. The vast majority of Indians are respectful, hospitable, and helpful. You'll find them to be delightful and intelligent travel companions.

HEALTH
India's Health
Despite decades of effort and education by both government and nonprofit sectors, huge strides in India's economy and technology, and the popularity of medicine as a profession, India is sadly among the world's leaders in child malnutrition, diabetes, tuberculosis, typhoid, and HIV/AIDS. It is still plagued by diseases like polio that have been eradicated elsewhere.

It seems impossible for infrastructures to keep pace with population. Good health care remains inaccessible to India's majority. Bad water, improper waste management, and air pollution result in nearly a million deaths each year. Low child immunization, increased travel, and overprescribing of antibiotics all contribute to the spread of communicable diseases.

In contrast, India has some excellent hospitals and highly qualified doctors, but staff and facilities are forced to work beyond their capacity as people seeking medical care pour in from distant villages or neighboring states where care is absent. Poor pay, poorly maintained hospitals and clinics, lack of advancement opportunity, and corruption discourage good doctors and nurses from providing care in needy rural areas and have pushed many of India's finest physicians to practice medicine outside India.

Even where health care is available, poverty and misconceptions about disease or healing prevent many people from going to doctors. Understanding of basic health issues such as proper nutrition or treating diarrhea is often derived from folk beliefs and remedies. Only 10 percent of the entire population carry health insurance. Medication can be had over the counter without a doctor's prescription, so many villagers and poor people simply self-diagnose or rely on their corner pharmacist for medical advice.

India's Medicine

A majority of people in India turn to the naturopathic Ayurvedic system of medicine to meet their basic medical needs. Ayurveda (Sanskrit, "life science") arose in India during the Vedic period and is written about in the ancient Hindu scriptures, the *Vedas*. Ayurveda defines health as balance, illness as imbalance. The three bodily energies, or *doshas* ("that which deteriorates"), of air, fire, and water can be set in order through eating foods based on body type, proper digestion, physical exercise, and yoga or meditation.

Siddha medicine is another popular system from Tamil Nadu. The Hindu god Shiva is said to have passed down the rules of proper balance of the three energies to his followers ("*siddhar*," those with extraordinary power), which cover dietary restrictions, the use of herbs, plants, metals, minerals, and chemicals, yoga, and meditation.

Homeopathy, a German form of alternative medicine, is also widely practiced in India.

Sanitation

The signs of India's sanitation problems can be seen—and smelled—everywhere. Trash and refuse are nonchalantly disposed of, handled only by certain low- or outcaste groups of people. Wandering cows, bulls, and goats serve as a cleanup crew, too, eating rotting vegetables tossed near the market. Pigs search side streets for human waste.

Public lavatories are not always available when you need one. Men merely need to find a wall, but women will find the lack of facilities difficult. In major cities it's best to look for a hotel or restaurant. Make use of clean places when you find them.

Food and Water

Many parasites, bacteria, and diseases, including hepatitis and typhoid (India's most common communicable disease), are waterborne. The easiest way to protect your health is by drinking only bottled water or bringing your own filter. Don't drink tap water or anything served with ice. When buying bottled water or soft drinks, check the cap to make sure it has not been previously opened. It's not uncommon for shopkeepers or *dhabbah-walas* to refill used bottles with tap water or homemade "soft drinks." Fruit juice may contain unfiltered water. So ask before ordering, or simply avoid them altogether. Use bottled water to brush your teeth, or brush without water.

It's not just ingested water that can make you sick. Pollution from water and food is more common during the monsoon. If you're in India at that time, beware of waterborne diseases. Rivers may not be safe to swim in. After heavy rain, streets will be flooded with dirty water. If you have to walk in flooded streets, bathe or dry off as soon as possible. Mosquitoes breed in standing water, which becomes a source of serious diseases, such as malaria and dengue fever. The high humidity in most of India promotes fungal growth on walls in homes and public buildings. Those suffering from asthma will need to take extra precautions and have inhalers or medication on hand.

There are common rituals and protocols observed in daily life that promote purity and, in fact, are good practices for staying healthy in the Indian context. As we have seen, nearly all Indians have clean and unclean foods. Even if you don't share their beliefs, these food restrictions have developed for a reason. Cooked vegetarian food is always the safest choice when you're eating out. Meat may not be fresh, especially at *dhabbahs* and in bus or train stations.

Diarrhea, or "loose motion" in India, is the most common problem for visitors to India. Make sure you drink plenty of clean water or fresh coconut water (in the shell). An Indian specialty, lime soda, made with either sugar or salt, is good for rehydration. Yogurt and *kichirdi* (rice cooked with lentils) can also help. You may want to seek local medical attention. Your doctor can prescribe antibiotics for you to take with you on your trip and use as needed, or you can buy them over the counter once you're in India.

Heat

The heat can affect you before you know it. To prevent heat exhaustion, cramps, or stroke, stay hydrated and stay indoors, limiting physical activity during the hot season. Heatstroke, which can be fatal, is characterized by increased body temperature, flushed skin, disorientation, and sometimes hallucinations and seizures. It requires immediate medical attention. See the Centers for Disease Control and Prevention (www.cdc.gov) for details regarding self-care in India's extreme temperatures.

HIV and Aids

Expats moving to India are required to take an AIDS test prior to receiving their visa, but the biggest problem is already inside India's borders. HIV once afflicted only the high-risk populations of prostitutes, truck drivers and other migrant workers, drug users, and those engaging in male homosexual activity. Now it affects people at every level of society. Of those diagnosed with HIV, 39 percent are women, most of whom have been infected by husbands involved in high-risk activities.

In the past twenty years India has invested heavily in AIDS awareness and prevention. Due to the stigma attached not only to AIDS but to behavior associated with it, people are reluctant to be tested. Many health workers in India are not aware of the dangers, either: the use of unsterilized needles by doctors as well as blood transfusions from infected donors remains one of the main factors cited for the spread of HIV.

Be Prepared

Before traveling to India, discuss immunization requirements and recommendations with your doctor at least six months in advance. You may need a series of injections over an extended period. Make sure you carry insurance information and phone numbers for your physician, an emergency contact back home, and a contact number in India, if possible. Find more information on current health risks and prevention at the Centers for Disease Control and Prevention and the World Health Organization (http://www.who.int/en).

SAFETY
Violence
Terror attacks, bombings, and kidnappings, sometimes targeting Westerners, are front-page news. Jammu Kashmir and the border between India and Pakistan have ongoing disputes that make travel to those places dangerous. Most of India's tensions are between castes or religious groups. The US State Department (http://travel.state.gov/) provides up-to-date information and travel warnings (British Foreign and Commonwealth Office: http://www.fco.gov.uk; Canadian Foreign Affairs and International Trade: http://www.voyage.gc.ca).

Restricted Areas
The Indian government requires special permission for both foreigners and Indians to visit certain parts of India, including the Andaman and Nicobar Islands, Lakshadweep (the Union Territory of the Laccadives Islands), many northeastern states, and some border regions.

Crime
Pickpocketing is common in and around tourist sites and public transportation. Keep valuables, documents and cash hidden on your person, and tuck cameras and other valuable items away in a theft-proof bag when not in use. Consider leaving expensive jewelry, such as an engagement ring, at home. As a foreigner you're an easy target for theft. If you must bring valuables, don't leave them in your hotel room. Put them in the hotel safe, if it has one.

Some foreigners, eager to trust people, unaware of cultural cues, or ignorant of popular scams, become targets for con artists and fraudsters. Never hand your passport to anyone, even official-looking people, on the street. Don't turn your back on any personal belongings unless they are chained down. Take multiple copies of your passport (first and last pages and the visa). Extra passport photos may also be required for certain forms once you're in India.

Special Advice for Women

You may simply be being friendly, but easy, open conversation, eye contact, and any kind of physical touch may well be interpreted as a come-on. If you are traveling alone, make friends with another woman or a family near you on the train or bus. Dress modestly, covering legs, arms, and cleavage.

An Indian man may ask to take your photograph, or to have his friend take your picture with him. Such pictures become the background for lies about his "new foreign girlfriend" or his latest sexual conquest. If you don't want to be fantasy material, don't allow your picture to be taken by men.

These things may irritate and anger you, as a woman who may not be accustomed to such treatment. But challenging the system by refusing to act in culturally appropriate ways will not change these men or this negative aspect of India.

Sexual assaults on women traveling alone are on the rise. Be aware of your surroundings and take sensible precautions. The best way to take care of yourself is to adjust to the cultural norms for women and surround yourself with good people—of whom, of course, there are plenty.

BUSINESS BRIEFING

Once viewed as a case study for third-world poverty or seen as an exotic destination for adventurous tourists, India is now the world's one-stop technology shop. Reforms over the past twenty years have liberalized foreign investment, reduced tariffs, opened up the financial sector, and deregulated industry. India has become a global giant, generating wealth and jobs, opening doors to new markets, and providing critical skills for the world economy.

Indian business acumen is nothing new. In 2000, according to a World Bank study, one million Indian-born people were living in the world's thirty wealthiest countries, not including India. India bemoaned the "brain drain" as many college-educated men and women left to pursue higher education or to join extended family and experience a higher standard of living abroad. Just a few years ago, Indians were the second-largest, and one of the fastest-growing, legal immigrant populations in the USA. But not any more.

Today, reverse immigration is motivated by the very things that spurred emigration in the past: better career opportunities, education and environment for children, and quality of life, along with a desire to reconnect with family and friends. Recent government initiatives make it easier for Indians who have relinquished their citizenship or who were born and raised abroad to invest money, start businesses, and to acquire a lifelong visa.

The reverse immigration of unprecedented numbers of young, competent, and highly educated Indians is also pushing US and European companies to shift their research and development to India. Many companies outsource technological services or move entire areas of business to India to retain the know-how and expertise being lost in the new migration, as well as to take advantage of the affordability of India's labor force.

These returnees, after years of living, studying, and working in the West, understand Western business practices and Western cultural values. That makes doing business in India more attractive. But corporate and government structures and policies, as well as deeper, usually unspoken values, create tensions that require cross-cultural skill, relational savvy, and additional investment of time and money on the part of the foreign business person.

BUSINESS CULTURE
Hierarchy
Indian business organization charts may look familiar, but there are overlapping structures based on family, caste, and other social dynamics that do not show up in the documentation.

The CEO and anyone with a recognized title will be given the respect due to their position, regardless of color, caste, or gender. Supervisors are respected and obeyed. Challenging ideas, contradicting opinions, questioning decisions, and saying "no" are not acceptable behavior for underlings. Considerable energy is expended on being agreeable to one's boss. Indians place a high value on pleasing those in authority. In a hierarchy, your position and well-being are contingent on those above you looking good and on those below you being controlled. Employees work hard to meet deadlines, to agree with their superiors, and to avoid making—or revealing—mistakes.

Indians painfully learn as children that they are not allowed to make mistakes. When a mistake happens, it is ignored if possible, hidden when necessary, and fixed at all costs before it can become public. In this shame-based culture, even trivial errors that have no economic fallout have emotional and relational consequences. Failures must be managed and minimized with excuses, blaming others, or blatant lies.

Networks

Networks are already established by the time a graduate looks for a job or an entrepreneur starts a business. Family and caste or community have supported and directed the individual from birth, and will continue to do so during their career. Relatives often work together. The majority of employees in a business may be from a single caste. It's not discrimination per se—it's the established support system at work.

It is also a kind of insurance. Financial assets, special skills, and even family secrets are kept within the family or community. In these homogeneous environments, the broader social ranking and internal family dynamics come into play, with clearly defined roles and predictable relationships. Relational entanglements and communal politics, however, can sabotage communication and productivity. Tensions may be felt but not understood by those outside the system.

> ### *COMMON MISTAKES FOREIGNERS MAKE IN BUSINESS RELATIONSHIPS*
> - Treating everyone as an equal.
> - Addressing people by their first names.
> - Greeting people with a hug or a kiss.
> - Offering a contrary opinion.
> - Publicly pointing out problems or conflicts in an attempt to solve them.
> - Initiating a discussion that requires debate or disclosure of weakness.
> - Assuming everyone understands your English.
> - Assuming you are getting all the facts.
> - Asking for decisions to be made during a meeting.
> - Using the same management tools as used in your home country.
> - Not including an allowance in project timelines for miles of red tape.
> - Offering or receiving money or important documents with the left hand.

Relationships and Time

The relaxed Indian view of time and the relational capital required to get things done should not be mistaken for laziness, carelessness, naivety, or ineptitude. You may feel time is wasted as conversations circle around many personal and professional issues, but work is being accomplished. Attempts to drive the discussion in a straight line will bring everything to a halt or, more likely, you will be carrying on a conversation with yourself while everyone else is moving in a different direction. Expect to spend time building relationships both with those who appear to have power and with those who do not.

Gatekeepers

In spite of a clear hierarchy, getting things done is not as simple as walking into the top office. A lot of time and effort are required to run around to various offices, fill out forms, get multiple signatures, and secure the goodwill of everyone in the process.

Gatekeepers can be found at every level. Some are gatekeepers by position, others by cunning. It could be the receptionist at the front desk, the clerk with the rubber stamp, the accountant whose signature is required, or the employee who has a relative who can get it done more cheaply. Even for many at the bottom of the food chain, their importance to the system is highlighted by their power to stall or sabotage the process. You will be asked to wait even if it is clear that the person has nothing else to do. You will be told to "come back tomorrow." Tomorrow, when you turn up, you will find the same person doing the same thing he could have completed yesterday.

Resist the urge to engage in a power struggle. As a foreigner you may be allowed to go directly to the boss, but it's best to show respect to everyone you meet on the way. At some point one of those gatekeepers will be the right person to get the job done or to influence others who can help you.

MEETINGS
Getting Started

E-mails, official memos, or other corporate forms of communication are not the most effective ways of setting up meetings or making important requests. Because of the relational nature of doing business in India, personal invitations or a phone call from the immediate supervisor are required.

Punctuality is relative and will depend on the expectations of the corporate leadership. People will arrive at meetings within a time frame understood as acceptable. In some cases, if an employee shows up within twenty minutes of the designated start time, no "excuse" is necessary.

Even at the height of the monsoon season or summer heat, Indians look clean and smart. Starched shirts and striped ties are standard business wear for men. Women are wrapped conservatively in perfectly pleated saris, *shalwar kameez*, or modest dresses. Be sure that you, too, are dressed appropriately when meeting businesspeople or making presentations.

At the Meeting

Indian business meetings, generally speaking, are more like presentations than forums for discussion or collaborative thinking. The senior member speaks his mind, and others seldom speak at all. It is not that they don't have anything to contribute: it is the right of those in authority to speak and the responsibility of others to listen. Indians do not interrupt those in authority. Silence is understood to be acquiescence. Any other response may be viewed as negative.

To contribute as an equal is to engage in a power struggle. Rarely will an employee risk putting his or her idea forward in a group setting. The danger of being shamed is too great. Even in a one-on-one conversation, aggressively pursuing a goal or a direct line of reasoning will create a problem, as one party will believe he has persuaded the other and the other party will be wondering how to get out of the deal without damaging the relationship.

Formal meetings are useful for disseminating information, affirming one's position of power, or communicating vision and instructions. They are not an effective way of generating ideas, understanding employee concerns, evaluating performance, gathering information, or getting real consensus. Rather, time and energy should be spent on regular, informal meetings with individuals.

In the Indian context, respect, listening, acknowledgment of contributions, specific expectations, and clear decisions are important. You may be able to make headway in a meeting by creating clear ground rules for discussion and contribution. But performance reviews, brainstorming sessions, and other Western management tools intended to strengthen performance, spur creative discussion, correct weaknesses, and build teams may do more harm than good. In the Indian business context communication is top-down, rather than lateral, and creativity and debate are not expected—or desired—in employees.

At the end of a meeting, clearly stated goals and action steps may be well received. But do not expect follow-through without a human connection that will ensure accountability. This is especially true if an employee is unsure of how to proceed, since they are not likely to admit ignorance or inability to a superior.

Presentations

At the climax of your presentation, when you might expect everyone to be applauding or getting out their checkbooks, you may look around the room to see blank stares and bobbing heads. No one has understood your British or American English and, afraid of embarrassing you and themselves, no one will say so. Because of the many ways in which communication can go awry, repetition and clarification of key points is essential. It is worth asking "Is my English clear?" at regular intervals during your presentation.

Younger urbanized Indians and those educated in the West may be better able to recognize variations in accents and to respond to a more direct, informal management style. But don't assume that superficially familiar behavior on their part, such as addressing you by your first name, or wearing jeans to the office, means that you are properly understood. Adaptations may be based on Western media images. Even those who may be more Westernized in their thinking are still part of a system built around an Indian frame of reference.

Decision Making

Decisions are made by the person with the appropriate title. As long as employees feel that their work is valued and their position is secure, they see no need to share the boss's responsibility. The person required to make the decision may consult peers, specialists, or family members to minimize the risk of making a bad decision or of taking the blame for it. Decisions are often based on the criteria of perceived trustworthiness and likeability rather than on competence and track record. And family and strategic relationships are always factors when hiring, promoting, or firing.

NEGOTIATIONS

If the person you're dealing with is not the decision maker, then more discussion, documentation, and protocols will be required to get appropriate approvals. Depending on your position, you may be able to go straight to the top—CEO to CEO or division manager to department head. But it's easy to misstep in a complicated hierarchy in which nepotism and caste or communal loyalties may be at work. Deals can go awry at any moment if you unknowingly circumvent someone in power, omit a signature, or choose the wrong go-between.

Expect negotiations and implementation to take much longer than they would at home. Rushing in, pushing agendas, directly addressing problems, or making demands will only alienate you from those who need to be involved in the process.

CONTRACTS

In India, a written contract may be regarded as fluid—open to adaptation when circumstances or personnel change. It may be viewed as an indicator of an intention established in the context of a prior relationship. Business colleagues, relying on their relationship with you rather than on a piece of paper, may be surprised if you raise an objection or threaten legal action if part of a contract has not been fulfilled. Past conversations may be offered as evidence that different arrangements were made by verbal agreement.

Indian contracts need careful attention on many levels. Though the language will be English, clarification may be needed because of differing word usage. Smaller companies may not use lawyers to draft or negotiate contracts, so that these can read very differently from the highly formal legal documents normal in the West. Different perceptions of what constitutes a key point can lead to confusing conversations, calling for patience and flexible thinking. A foreign company will need to establish clearly the specific laws that govern a contract and its arbitration. For matters relating to intellectual property, "work for hire," liability, and taxes you will need the help of a qualified lawyer.

CORRUPTION

Corruption continues to plague India. Despite the economic reforms, India's huge bureaucracies create barriers that many choose to overcome by means of bribery. Red tape can make registering a company, getting a tax ID number, or dealing with banks a slow and infuriating process. Obstinate officials may extort *baksheesh* to move your request forward or to turn on standard services, such as electricity. Kickbacks, from a designer watch or a night with a prostitute to a multimillion dollar payoff, are widespread in government, education, and business. Though policemen and politicians are the worst culprits, educational institutions receive the highest percentage of payoffs as people compete for admission.

India pays a high price for these practices. The Indian entrepreneur, corporate strategist, and University of Michigan business professor C. K. Prahalad estimates that corruption costs India more than US $20 trillion a year. Sadly, a bribe is often more expedient and less confusing than the hassle that can be created by clerks, bureaucrats, police officers, government officials, and school administrators. While such "tips," bribes, and gifts are not the only way to get things done, you and your company will have to decide how to handle this common facet of "business as usual" in India.

COLLEAGUES
Day-to-Day Communication
Ask colleagues how best to stay in touch. E-mail, which may be the preferred means of communication back home, may only be checked intermittently by your Indian associates, who may be more used to phone conversations.

Communication should be direct and personal. Official paper reports or e-mail communications will probably convey what you want to hear rather than what's actually being done. Face-to-face is best. When that's not possible, Skype or telephone contact can help build or maintain the relational capital needed to get the job done.

Working Together

"Able to work independently" is not something you're likely to see on a job description in India. Competence matters, but dependability and loyalty matter more. Employees may be expected to help one another to complete work by deadlines or to provide skills or connections that are lacking. Decisions are rarely made alone. Consulting and consensus protect an employee from being blamed when a decision leads to failure. Colleagues want to know that their workmates can be counted on to help them succeed, to make them look good to superiors, and to cover for them when mistakes are made.

While many have the drive to excel and everyone wants to be acknowledged for work done well, to be singled out for attention, even when it's positive, creates difficulties. For example, giving a raise based on performance, rather than seniority, may create dissatisfaction in the ranks. High performers may have to deal with their colleagues' jealousy, which can damage relationships and prospects.

These and other stressful aspects of Indian business culture can stifle initiative and independent thought. On the other hand they have compelled frustrated and enterprising individuals to strike out on their own, creating new businesses and greater opportunity for many.

MANAGING CONFLICT

Two words are the key here: conflict avoidance. As we have seen, transparency is difficult, if not impossible, to find. Indians do not criticize others to their face. Ideas are not challenged. Differences of opinion are not voiced. You will hear what they think you want to hear. Even if you ask for honest input you probably won't get it, especially if it is deemed to be negative or conflict-laden.

Most Indians appreciate practical Western problem solving, organizational skills, and a "can-do" attitude; but those same qualities can create tension. If you step into a workplace to identify problems or suggest ways to enhance efficiency, you may be perceived as arrogant, thoughtless, and rude. If colleagues are silent or reluctant to take action, do not mistake this for incompetence, apathy, or lack of confidence. Rifts can widen because no one will risk the relationship to address tensions.

It may be possible to have a conversation about conflict in the workplace if this is done privately. Be humble about your role and honest about your desire for resolution. Assure your colleagues that you will not use what they say against them. If they trust you they may open up. If not, change your strategy. Listen to what they say about others for clues about their values, their pressure points, their expectations, and, perhaps, how these relate to you. Then it's up to you to adjust your expectations and behavior.

WOMEN IN BUSINESS

There are strong, capable women at all levels of business and government in India. In 2005, 10 percent of the country's entrepreneurs were women. Even so, the pressures of family obligations, fears of sexual harassment, and assumptions about limitations prevent many from being employed in some professions, or offered advancement, or even entering the marketplace.

Generally women in business are treated with respect, but there are few Indian women in upper management positions. Western women tend to be treated more as a male peer might be. Depending on the company, and those in authority, women doing business in India may well enlist male help to communicate, negotiate, and ensure implementation of decisions. India's relational and hierarchical style of doing business requires the kind of one-on-one conversation and socializing that's still not possible between the sexes in India.

COMMUNICATING

LANGUAGE

Language Families and Factions

Experts differ on the number of languages spoken in India. Officially, the government recognizes twenty-two, but 2,000 have been identified. Most Indian languages derive from two linguistic families—Indo–Aryan and Dravidian. Hindi in its various forms comes from Indo–Aryan-based Sanskrit, and is the primary language of 70 percent of India's people. The Dravidian-based languages of South India—Tamil, Telugu, Malayalam, and Kannada—are spoken by 26 percent. The rest, heard in the northeast and on India's islands, are unrelated Sino–Tibetan and Austro–Asiatic languages.

Hindi was made India's "official" (though not national) language in India's constitution in 1950, and English was to continue as "an associate official language" for fifteen years. Today English is still commonly used in business, and is the preferred medium of education, especially for the middle and upper classes.

More recently, regions and states have asserted their linguistic rights and cultural identities by reassigning original names to their major cities. Calcutta is now Kolkata (Bengali); Bombay is Mumbai (Marathi); Bangalore is Bangaluru (Kannada); Madras is Chennai (Tamil); and Pondicherry is Puducherry (Tamil). Other name changes are being considered.

Strong feelings come out in discussions on India's languages. Most educated Indians speak two, if not three, four, or five languages; but each feels passionately about his or her mother tongue.

HINDI WORDS AND PHRASES

Accha	Good, OK, or really?
Dhanyavad	Thank you
Maaf kijiye	I'm sorry
Namaste	Hello; literally, "I recognize the divine in you"
Tik hai	It's fine, or I'm fine
Wala	One associated with, or who does, something (*chai wala*, tea-maker)
Shabaash!	Excellent!—a word of congratulations or praise

Whose English?

The history of politics and education combined with current global business opportunities have motivated Indians to continue to learn to read, write, and speak English—but this may be a different English from yours.

Indian children are still taught the King's English. Educated Indians have excellent English and can be very articulate. But Indian English, evolved during the British Raj, has some idiosyncrasies.

English and its Indian variants are spoken or written not just on the job or in the club, but on TV, in movies, and in contemporary literature. There are purists who argue for a return to precolonial languages, but the English tsunami hit India long ago, and waves of Indian English, or "Hinglish," and IT-trained Americanisms and accents continue to pour into India.

IT'S INDIAN ENGLISH, ISN'T IT?

Isn't it?	Isn't that the case? (at the end of a sentence)
Tell me	I'm listening, or Can I help you?
I'll try	I can't (but I don't want to hurt your feelings).
Yes	No (in answer to questions stated in the negative: "Aren't you going?" or "Didn't you do it?" "Yes" (I am not going, or I didn't do it)."
What to do?	Nothing can be done about it
Off it	Turn it off
Good name	Full name
Out of station	Out of town
Healthy	Fat
Hotel	Restaurant
Prepone	Move an appointment earlier
Shifting	Moving
Simply	Just, or just like that

Language Learning

Most people in urban India speak at least basic English. But, because of the inextricable link between language and identity, any effort you make to learn a few basic phrases will be appreciated by those you meet. Communication, not perfection, is the goal. So ask questions, take a few linguistic risks, laugh at and learn from your mistakes. Enjoy the beauty of India's languages and the people who speak them.

There are some excellent language-learning tools available. Many universities offer classes, and students, teachers, or others can be hired as tutors. Almost anyone will be willing to teach you a phrase or two, and to correct your pronunciation. Over time, TV and movies will add to your ability to listen, to comprehend, and to speak.

GREETINGS

In this traditional society, how you greet others matters. Respect, relationship, religion, and social status are communicated in greetings.

In many arenas today handshakes, especially between men, are acceptable. With a woman, it's best to use the traditional "*Namaste*" or "Hello" with the hand posture and a smile (see box overleaf). Only shake her hand if she extends it first. Europeans and Americans should not greet members of the opposite sex with a kiss or a hug.

BODY LANGUAGE

Trying to read body language and watch social cues in India can exasperate an outsider. Much of what is communicated is nonverbal. It's easy to misunderstand, or to miss something altogether. If you think you've missed something important, ask an Indian to explain; but they've probably read the situation without having to think about it, so they may not know what you're talking about.

Don't be confused by the side-to-side head bob. You may think someone is shaking their head to mean "no," but it means "yes," or "I hear you," and sometimes "thank you."

Finger pointing is rude. Gesturing in a direction is done either with the chin or by using the whole hand. To sign to someone to come to you, hold your hand palm down and wave your fingers. Beckoning with palm up is inappropriate, as are winking, whistling, and singing, which can be interpreted as sexual come-ons.

Signs of Respect

Signs of respect are important in India. Women may be expected to cover their heads when entering religious places or if they are present when prayers are being said in someone's home. Not making direct eye contact is a sign, too, to elders that you are giving them due respect. Shoes are unclean. Never put them on a table or other furniture. Removing shoes to enter a home or a holy place is a given. You may choose to keep your socks on, if you're wearing any, but bare feet are the norm. Sometimes a shoe or a *chappal* (sandal) is used by a woman to threaten a man who is doing something shameful.

COMMON GREETINGS AND GESTURES
North Indian Hindus
"*Namaste.*" Place palms together, with hands held in front of your chest. (You don't need to bow—it's not done in India.) The hand gesture alone is a respectful greeting, especially when you enter a roomful of people.

Pranam is a more formal gesture that you'll observe in north India. With fingertips, one touches the feet of a parent, elder family member, or other respected person. It is often followed by putting one's hand on one's heart or head, acknowledging that this person has the power to bless.

South Indians
"Hello" is "*Namaskara*" (Kannada), "*Namasakaram*" (Malayalam, Telugu), or "*Vanakham*" (Tamil), accompanied by the traditional "*namaste*" hand gesture, handshake, or briefly touching hand to chest.

Muslims
"*Assalaam alaikum*" ("peace be upon you")
Reply: "*Alaikum salaam*" ("upon you be peace")

HUMOR

One needs only to look at Indian cinema to begin to grasp the place of humor in India and to see what Indians find funny. From broad physical comedy to subtle verbal exchanges or offhand remarks, even serious Indian films are laced with laughs. Slapstick and parody are typically what foreigners understand as "Indian humor," since other forms of humor and its nuances cannot be understood without knowing the language and learning the culture.

It may appear that nothing is sacred in Indian comedy. Social relationships, subcultures, caste and class, social ills, holy men, physical traits—all are mocked and satirized by comedians in film, on TV, in comedy clubs, and by groups of young people just having fun. With the increase of NRIs (nonresident Indians) and second and third generations living outside the country, Indian comedy has begun to express their cross-cultural realities and internal struggles.

Not all humor translates across cultures. There are forms of humor to avoid if you don't want to be misunderstood. Sarcasm will certainly offend. Self-deprecating humor will be viewed as a statement of fact about yourself that may return to haunt you.

Trying to ease tension by making light of a person or problem will be interpreted as a put-down. Although many cultures have jokes about specific subcultures, Sardar (Sikh) jokes, the Indian equivalent of "blonde" jokes in the USA, are best avoided. Caricature is a common form of comedy in film and even between friends, but Indians do not poke fun at or joke around with parental figures, bosses, or anyone deemed above them in the social order.

MEDIA AND TECHNOLOGY

Not only interpersonal and business relationships, but lifestyle and culture are changing radically as India's consumers and companies connect globally to goods, education, business, and opportunities in and through technology. India is now the largest provider of IT outsourcing in the world and the fastest-growing market for technology-related goods and services.

The Press
Not everything has been taken over by technological advances. While the West turns from the printed page to TV and the Internet, most Indians still get their news from

newspapers. India's newspaper circulation of 59 million is topped only by that of Japan and China. Printing presses roll out 62,000 newspapers, including 5,000 dailies, in more than a hundred languages. India's largest daily newspaper is *Dainik Jagran*, a Hindi publication servicing most of North India. With 17 million copies sold a day, its readership is estimated to be more than 55 million.

The Indian press is independent and privately owned. Editors and TV chiefs appear to exercise self-censorship and intentionally minimize crises and underestimate the numbers injured and dead in a conflict in efforts to prevent the escalation of further violence.

Air Waves
Only 32 percent of Indian families own TV sets, and there are 116 million radios—one for every ten Indians. In this interconnected and highly social society, neighbors and relatives often watch or listen to special programs or sports events together.

In the past Indian television was dominated by Doordarshan, India's government-owned TV station, which used the cultural love for the arts and visual media, and the tendency of the uneducated in India to perceive what they saw on the small screen as reality, to promote certain political views. But in 1990 the Prasar Bharati Act required an independent Broadcasting Corporation to be established to regulate both TV and radio broadcasting.

A year later, satellite TV exploded on to the Indian TV scene. Now more than 560 TV stations broadcast across India, including forty domestic news agencies. Sports, soaps, religious sagas, contests, dramas, comedies, and news programs are available in every major language. British and American TV shows are popular.

Internet

India is wired. The proliferation of outsourcing companies, IT businesses, computer training centers, and Internet cafés indicates the e-change that's happening.

In the world, India ranks fourth in Internet use, despite the low number of PC owners. Networks exist in and around major cities, but connections can be sketchy or just plain slow. Electricity is still a problem in India. Nearly half the population has no electricity, and those who do have it frequently experience frustrating outages.

Still, Internet access is a welcome development for visitors who can connect with people back home, or with business colleagues and traveling companions. If you plan to stay in India more than three days, you are allowed to bring in one laptop without paying customs fees. If you carry a laptop or handheld device, remember to take an adaptor that fits Indian 230 volt, 50 Hz outlets. USB-based Wi-Fi devices are available from several carriers inside India at a modest price. But if you need repairs, service centers outside the major cities will be hard to find.

Telephone

Until 1994 telecommunications was a government monopoly. Bharat Sanchar Nigam Limited (BSNL), as the government-owned company is now known, is still a major service provider, with more than 57 million customers. State governments continued to hold on to international calling facilities until 1999, but turn-of-the-century policy changes ushered in a new era of communication in India.

India is the largest seller of cell phone connections and the world's fastest-growing market. According to India's Telecoms Regulatory Authority, there are nearly 300 million telephones, 70 percent of them in urban areas. Wireless subscribers number 250 million. Nine million new phones enter the market every month. Cell phones are relatively affordable and accessible, and pundits predict that in the next few years there will be a billion Indian cell phone users.

Public Call Offices (PCOs, also known as STD or ISO) used to be the only option for phone calls. They are still popular, with more than 900,000 PCOs providing calling services in India. Pay phones for local calls can be found in restaurants, grocery stores, and other public places. Prepaid phones and SIM cards are readily available.

Mail

India Post boasts the world's largest number of post offices in the world. Its 155,000 offices, most of which are located outside the cities, also serve as banks for rural India. In the past decade, increased competition and use of technology are pushing the Post Office to update and improve its services.

Speed post, money orders, bill payment, and international fund transfers (including e-payment) can all be done at the post office. "EPost" is a recent addition to services. Customers can have an e-mail sent to a post office in the destination city, where it will be printed and delivered to the recipient by snail mail. Though the volume of mail has decreased in recent years, India Post still delivers 6.3 billion pieces of mail annually. As with all government offices in India, service will depend on holidays, "*bandhs*" (political protests), and strikes.

CONCLUSION

All descriptions of "India" or "Indians" can only be offered as a simplification to aid understanding, rather than as a complete representation. That's both the beauty and the challenge of visiting India—there is little that can be labeled generically as "Indian culture." And there is little that compares with our own life "back home," at least beyond the superficial trappings assumed under the influence of the British Raj and MTV.

India has conquered conquerors, illuminated artists, inspired sages, spawned invention, and is today changing the face and the future of our world. Indians have a joke about the extent of their influence, saying that when the first spaceship landed on the moon, the astronauts heard "*Chai! Chai!*" and stepped out to find an Indian selling tea from a cart. That is a good picture of the reality of India: still doing things the old way yet paradoxically far ahead of everyone else.

Daily life for most is still patterned after the routine of previous generations, focused on caring for family and, if fate allows, preparing one's children for a better future. Fatalism and the synthesis of the Hindu concepts of *karma* (we get what we deserve) and *maya* (what we see is not real) into all of India's cultures give Indians a capacity to live with social inequity and personal hardship without having to manage it, excuse it, or pretend it isn't there.

Life is made both difficult and predictable by the still dominant system of caste. Everyone knows their place, and options are determined by community, gender, and the social pecking order. But in ways that were unthinkable a generation ago those barriers are being surmounted. Doors to education and a better future are slowly being opened by law, economic reform, globalization, technological advancement, media, and a seismic culture shift that is just beginning to shake India's ancient footing.

The intensity and diversity of India can create both shock and awe for visitors that are not likely to subside. India is an experience best appreciated by those who are open to learn, able to cope with ambiguity, and willing to redefine generosity and friendship. Falling in love with India is much like developing a taste for spicy food. You look at the chilies and don't know how you'll cope. But the aroma is enticing, so you dive in. If you don't give up, one day you'll discover that you've developed a craving for it.

India of the ages is not dead, nor has she spoken her last creative word; she lives and has still something to do for herself and the human peoples.
Sri Aurobindo

Further Reading

There is a vast range of books on every conceivable aspect of India.
Here are a few titles to start with.

Abram, David, et al. *The Rough Guide to India.*
London: Rough Guides, 2001.

Kalsi, Sewa Singh. *Sikhism.*
London: Simple Guides, 2007.

Kingsland, Venika Mehra. *Hinduism.*
London: Simple Guides, 2008.

Lewis, Richard D. *When Cultures Collide: Managing Successfully Across Cultures.* London: Nicholas Brealey Publishing, 1999.

O'Reilly, James P., and Larry Habegger (eds.). *India.*
San Francisco, California: Travelers' Tales, 1995.

Singh, Sarina, et al. *Lonely Planet: India.*
Melbourne/Oakland/London/Paris: Lonely Planet Publications, 2000.

Tammita-Delgoda, SinhaRaja. *A Traveller's History of India.*
Moreton-in-Marsh, Gloucestershire: Windrush Press, 1994;
Northampton, Mass.: 1994; London: Cassell, 2002.

Complete Hindi. New York: Living Language, 2007

culture smart! india

Index

Acknowledgments

Many thanks to: Mom for faith; Jo for confidence; Geoffrey for kindness; friends and colleagues for insight; Josh for companionship and comic relief; my Indian family for allowing me to belong; and Roy (you know what for). And to my fan club (you know who you are) who promised to buy and use my book. Here it is!